Max Allen
crush

Max crush
Allen

Photographs by Adrian Lander

TheNew
Australian
WineBook

mitchell beazley

Crush
by Max Allen

First published in Great Britain in 2000
by Mitchell Beazley, an imprint of
Octopus Publishing Group Ltd
2 -4 Herron Quays
London E14 4JP

Produced by Hardie Grant Books
12 Claremont Street
South Yarra 3141
Australia

ISBN 1 840 003 243

Edited by White Kite Productions
Cover and text design Mary Callahan
Maps by Guy Holt
Printed and bound by Tien Wah Press (PTE) in Singapore

Max and Ady would like to thank Tracy O'Shaughnessy and the team at Hardie Grant and Mitchell Beazley for having faith in the book and doing the best job putting it together; Mary Callahan for designing it with such verve and passion; Sally Moss for editing it so tightly; Guy Holt for making the maps so clear; everyone at Lab X for their excellent service and support with the photos; all of the photography assistants who helped Ady on this epic book: Jason, Katy, Alex and anyone else he's left out; and the Tasmanian and southern Queensland tourism authorities for help with travel. But most of all, we'd like to thank the good people who make up the Australian wine industry for their remarkable generosity, hospitality, patience and support – thankyou for putting us up and putting up with us.

Acknowledgements

To Sophie
and
To Adair

Contents

A Sense of Place
Australia's Wine Regions & Winemakers 78

From Aeroplane to Zinfandel 236
Australian Wine Words Unplugged

Introduction

I have spent the last ten years of my life soaking in Australian wine. Absolutely immersed in it up to my eyeballs. Ever since my first taste of good shiraz in a cool Clare Valley cellar door in 1990, I just haven't been able to get enough of the stuff. I have been obsessed.

At first, my obsession led me into wine shops and made me ask for a job, just so I could be there, standing amid the object of my affection all day. Then it took a back seat as I did the hard yards at a drive-through bottle shop in an inner Melbourne suburb, selling slabs of beer to big hairy blokes in beaten-up old Holden Kingswoods and bottles of cheap chardonnay to students on their way to the local Indian BYO.

My obsession drove me out to the nearest wine region to work vintage, lugging hoses around, picking grapes at dawn on a hillside that felt like a cliff face, shovelling skins and stalks out from behind the back of the crushing machine, getting hot and sticky – and fit, for once in my life. The obsession kept me at one winery for a couple of years, working behind the counter at cellar door, talking and tasting and being nice to people I didn't know.

My obsession also took me along to tastings, those weird events where people stand around a room sniffing and slurping and spitting wine into buckets and scribbling notes on backs of envelopes and looking dead serious and not talking to each other or smiling.

But this wasn't enough. I had to get closer to Australian wine, to spend even more of my time thinking about it, talking about it, drinking it.

I know, I thought, I'll 'blag' my way into becoming a wine writer. That sounds like a bit of a giggle. So I sent a story in to 'Epicure', the food and drink section of Melbourne's *Age* newspaper, and was absolutely staggered when they printed it. I wrote another one, and another one, and then managed to persuade somebody to publish a book about wine and … well, it's all been a little hazy since then.

It worked though. I now spend an inordinate amount of time travelling around Australia, tasting, drinking, talking, eating and soaking up even more of the wonderful wine experiences this vast country has to offer.

When I'm not travelling I'm opening bottles and tasting what's inside and two-finger typing newspaper articles about Australian wine and magazine features about Australian wine – and books like this about Australian wine. Finally, my obsession is satisfied.

Well, almost. You see, I've found this nice block of land that would be perfect for growing shiraz, just two hours' drive away, and a mate of mine wants to set up a small winery so I reckon if I planted, oh, I don't know, say two hectares to start off with, then expand to four in a few years …

This book has been written for anybody who feels the obsession coming on. Actually, it's a blatant attempt to enthusiastically encourage that obsession.

Like in my first book, *Red and White: Wine Made Simple*, there are no vintage charts, no star ratings, no graphs, no diagrams here (there *are* a couple of maps, but we couldn't do without them – and they are rather lovely maps). Like *Red and White* I didn't want to turn this into an encyclopaedia, or an atlas, or a buying guide to Australian wine.

Instead, what I want to do with this book is introduce you to the flavours, the stories, the places, the culture of Australian wine by distilling what I've tasted and seen over the last ten years, and splashing that essence all over the page. I want to make you feel as though you're standing among the vines watching grapes being picked, rich sun pouring down onto the back of your neck. I want to take you driving down a dead-straight highway in the gathering gloom of twilight to get to a remote but beautiful vineyard. I want to watch your face as you taste the first wine of the new vintage, its vibrant, lively fruit flavours dancing all over your tongue. I want to buy you a beer in a country pub after a long day's cellar door-hopping.

Once again, photographer Adrian Lander is my co-conspirator in the quest to get you more obsessed. We have travelled to every grape growing corner of this huge country, camera in one hand, trusty laptop in the other, eating and drinking, driving and flying, snapping and tapping and tasting like mad to try and capture the spirit of Australian wine.

I hope we've succeeded.

Max Allen

The Story
of Wine in
Australia

From 1788 to 2025

Open any international wine encyclopaedia published in the last twenty years or so and you'll probably find Australia up the back, lumped together with California, New Zealand, South America and South Africa under the heading 'New World'.

New World. Makes it sound like the whole shebang sprang up some time in the mid 1970s, doesn't it? Like Glam Rock, or something. This has always amused me because it couldn't be further from the truth. Scratch the surface of the Australian wine industry and you'll find it's saturated with a remarkably rich history that stretches across four centuries.

I realise the word *history* may either cause your eyes to glaze over or send you into a cold sweat (remember desperately trying to dredge up the names of early twentieth century prime ministers?), so I want to put your mind at rest. This chapter is not a comprehensive, fully detailed, statistical history of wine in Australia. That's been done elsewhere, at length and with far more serious erudition than I can muster. I wouldn't want to write that kind of history anyway.

I'd much rather do what I've tried to do here: put Australian wine into some kind of living, breathing context for you by conjuring up the people, places and flavours that have contributed to its development. So this quick ride on the roller-coaster of Australian wine history won't turn you into a wine academic, but it may help you become a more passionate wine drinker – because every time you open a bottle and drink a glass, you're drinking history.

One of the first things you learn when you start immersing yourself in the stories of wine in Australia is that there really is nothing new under the sun. All the big issues that define the Australian wine scene at the beginning of the twenty-first century – fleetingly fashionable wine styles, unstoppable exports, massive vineyard expansions, that kind of thing – have bubbled up (and then disappeared) at least once already over the last 200-odd years. This is the second thing you learn: the wine industry is not a static one; it changes dramatically, often when you least expect it. Which immediately leads us to the third lesson: very few Australian winemakers have ever paid any attention to the first two lessons.

Right now, the Australian wine industry is booming. There are more wineries, more vines in the ground and more wine being produced each year than there have been at any point in the country's history. But I'm leaping ahead of myself. Let's go right back to the beginning, to a hot eighteenth-century summer's evening in Sydney Cove, just a few weeks after the First Fleet, full of convicts, set foot on a distant continent on the other side of the earth.

Sydney, New South Wales, 1788

There's a glass of rum on the table. It's a rough, simple glass, designed to withstand the knocks and spills of an eight-month sea voyage. It's a simple table, too, knocked up out of a couple of chests and a hastily-sawn slab of gum tree. The last of the day's heavy sunlight and the first of the night's cicada drone filter through the tent canvas as Captain Arthur Phillip, the first governor of this new colony, picks up the glass and swigs it back.

It's been a busy day in the governor's garden. The few grapevine rootlings that survived the journey were planted out today in a freshly cleared patch of land, joining fruit trees and vegetables. The vines weren't the most important cargo on board – nowhere near as important as sheep (and people) – but Phillip is keen to see these plants succeed, like many other pioneers who are to follow him.

In some ways it seems pretty weird that vines were on board the First Fleet in the first place. After all, Great Britain doesn't exactly have the most vibrant history of winemaking. Sheep, apples, hops, wheat, yes – but the grapevine? How did this thoroughly continental plant manage to hitch a ride on a British adventure to the New World?

The explanation's easy. Although the British in the eighteenth century weren't winemakers, they most certainly were wine drinkers and wine merchants. And drinkers and merchants are always after a constant supply of cheap wine. At the time, many hoped that Australia would turn out to be England's vineyard: despite the huge distances, and despite the fact that it was primarily a convict settlement, the new colony was, after all, an outpost of the Empire (some Poms – and some Australians – think it still is).

Phillip's first little vineyard didn't survive, but a mob of others persisted on plots further inland in the hot colony of New South Wales, and by the beginning of the nineteenth century the embryo of an industry had come into existence.

London, England, 1823

There's a glass of fairly pale red wine sitting nervously on a mahogany table, surrounded by the serious-looking gentlemen of the Royal Society of Arts. One of the gentlemen picks up the glass, peers into it, takes a sniff,

then a sip, rolls it around his gums and lets it slip down his throat. Then he raises a bushy eyebrow and smiles faintly.

This is one of the first times a wine from the young colony of New South Wales has been tasted in England. It was sent by Gregory Blaxland from his vineyard near Parramatta, west of Sydney. It was made from 'burgundy' grapes (probably pinot noir), and had a dash of spirit added to fortify it for the long, rough journey. It is awarded a silver medal of encouragement.

Getting approval (and, eventually, orders) from the mother country was very important to the colony's earliest winemakers. With a population of only a few thousand, most of whom vastly preferred rough rum, Australia in the early nineteenth century was hardly gasping for table wine. Indeed, it wouldn't be until the 1850s and the discovery of gold that the local population swelled to anything resembling a market to sell to.

Not that this stopped the growing number of wine-obsessed pioneers, mind you: accounts of early figures like John McArthur and James Busby make them sound like near-religious fanatics, zealously extolling the virtues of the vine to anybody who'd listen. It was an enthusiasm made up of almost equal parts evangelism (table wine was seen as a civilising influence on the unruly masses in a land run by rum) and hard-nosed commercial interest (we could make a pile of cash flogging this booze to the Brits, chaps), and it was catching.

Something that doesn't always come through quite so strongly in the historical accounts, though, is how young and incredibly self-assured these pioneers often were. When Busby landed in Sydney in 1824 he was only twenty-four, yet he arrived clutching the manuscript for his book *A Treatise on the Culture of the Vine*, written specifically for (and hugely influential among) New South Welsh winegrowers. Just six years later, Busby had not only established one of the Hunter Valley's first vineyards but also imported an incredible collection of hundreds of different vines from Europe.

We usually see pictures of blokes like Busby in their twilight years – heavily whiskered, ruddy-faced – if they can afford to commission portrait artists, that is. But when they started out, when they were doing the hard yards, pursuing their big dreams, they were young fellas.

There's a glass of crystal clear, faintly golden wine sitting on a table in Joseph Gilbert's cool stone Pewsey Vale cellars in the wild and windswept Eden Valley. The visitor who has come to inspect Pewsey Vale for a book he is writing on the colony's vineyards takes the glass, examines it, sniffs and sips. The smile of recognition and admiration is broad. This is an extraordinary wine. Its fruit flavour is fragrant, delicate, pure. It is as good as – no, better than – a good riesling from Germany.

During the 1850s and early 60s, things really began humming for Australian wine. In South Australia, in the large vineyards around Adelaide, in the Barossa Valley to the north and McLaren Vale to the south, entrepreneurs started what were to become enduring wine estates. There was Doctor Penfold, doling out strong port from his surgery among the vines at Magill. There was Joseph Seppelt, arriving in Adelaide from Germany with half his village in tow, and heading out to the Barossa Valley to found a dynasty. There was Samuel Smith, turning his hand from brewing to winemaking at his new Yalumba winery near Angaston.

In Victoria, too, things were happening on a grand scale: big wineries were established by a gang of young Swiss aristocrats in the Yarra Valley, while the gold-rich areas of Rutherglen and Great Western saw vineyards spring up like companion crops to the mullock heaps.

The scale of these developments really was staggering. The winery buildings often resembled castles or grand mansions – or small towns. The vineyards stretched for miles across the country, thick blankets of green draped over hillside after hillside. There was a sense that anything was possible in the boom time.

This boom was funded mostly by gold. Victoria's central, western and northern wine regions, for example, were established because they happened to be close to the frenzied goldfields of the 1850s, rather than because of any far-sighted viticultural research. The fact that they produced good wine, and were to remain wine regions, was often accidental.

The vineyards stretched for miles across the country, thick blankets of green draped over hillside after hillside.

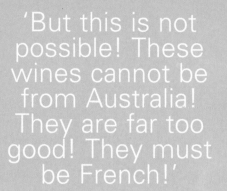

One of my favourite stories from this period tells of a panel of distinguished wine judges (all European, of course) at the Vienna International Exhibition in 1873. They have spent the morning working their way through the exhibits from France – Burgundy, Bordeaux, the Rhone. Now it's time to taste the red 'hermitage' (shiraz) wines from Australia.

The first bottle is opened and poured, then the ruby liquid is solemnly sniffed and slurped. Silence descends. A second bottle is sampled. The murmurs begin. A third and a fourth make their way round the table, until finally one of the judges blurts out: 'But this is not possible! These wines cannot be from Australia! They are far too good! They must be French!' It wasn't to be the last time that the quality of Australian wine shone on the international stage.

Such success was seen by many as a key to unlock the European wine markets, and by the end of the 1860s, people like Patrick Auld, from the Auldana vineyard in Adelaide (just across the road from Dr Penfold's Magill vineyard) had set up offices in London. It was the beginning of an ongoing commercial relationship between the two countries that expanded and contracted over the next century like a big fat pair of lungs.

Geelong, Victoria, 1882

Charles Tetaz takes another sip from his glass of pinot noir, a good, bright, red-coloured wine, and tries to choke back the tears. In front of him, all down the slopes of his twenty-five-year-old Prince Albert vineyard, workers are ripping vines from the ground and burning them. The vine louse phylloxera, which is busy munching its way through most of the vineyards of Europe, was discovered in Geelong in 1877. And the government of the day has reacted by destroying the industry faster than the louse ever could have.

Every silver lining has a cloud, and in the case of the Victorian wine industry the cloud was phylloxera, followed by financial collapse in the 1890s, followed by a change in public tastes away from the lighter, more European styles produced in cooler places such as the Yarra Valley, towards warm, strong, fortified wines and spirits. Phylloxera also polished off the early New South Wales vineyards.

Every cloud has a silver lining, though, and in the case of the South Australian industry, that silver lining was England. At the turn of the century and for another two decades, the Poms lapped up all the big, rich, 'tonic burgundies' and 'ferruginous' McLaren Vale reds they could lay their hands on. Strongly alcoholic, dark and full-bodied, these wines made the fortune of producers such as Thomas Hardy and merchants such as the London-based Peter Burgoyne. Even though Rutherglen, in north-east Victoria, was badly affected by phylloxera, its ability to also churn out beefy reds (and, as the market changed again, excellent fortifieds) kept it alive.

Towards the end of the century, the thirty-year-old Victorian politician Alfred Deakin (future prime minister and architect of Federation) took a step that would dramatically alter the course of Australian wine history (dramatic drum roll) when he invited the Californian Chaffey brothers to develop an irrigation system up around the vast River Murray in the north of the state. The Chaffeys eventually started their scheme across the border, in South Australia, but before long the irrigation has spread back into Victoria, effectively turning desert into farmland.

In 1912 a similar scheme brought water from the Murrumbidgee River to the arid lands around Griffith in New South Wales, and over the next half-century returned servicemen, battling farmers and Italian migrants would turn these fertile stretches of land into the steady beating heart of the modern Australian wine industry.

Manchester, England, 1932

There's a small glass of port on the table in the corner of the smoky public bar. Well, that's not strictly true. The strong, tawny, fortified wine in the

glass is called port, but it's not 'real' port, from Portugal. It's Australian 'port'. Not that that accurate nomenclature bothers anybody in this pub. They're drinking this strong wine like it's going out of fashion.

Which it wasn't. Thanks to a preferential tax on 'Empire' wines, the Poms imported more Australian wine than French wine during the 1930s, and thanks to convoluted excise regulations concerning alcohol content, the vast majority of it was fortified, like this port.

Much of this wine – and most of the spirit used to fortify it – came from the new irrigation areas, where it was usually produced by newly formed growers' co-operatives. A lot also hailed from the warm and highly productive Swan Valley in Western Australia, where Yugoslav refugees had settled before and during the First World War. Some high-quality table wines were being produced – Rudi Kronberger's early-bottled rieslings from Yalumba in the Barossa, a trickle of great reds from Bill Redman's winery in the as-yet-unrecognised or -exploited Coonawarra – but mostly the 1930s and 40s were the time of sherry, port and muscat.

Hunter Valley, New South Wales, 1945

Maurice O'Shea draws a sample of red wine from the old oak cask, squirts it into a small glass and squints at it through his thick specs. He takes a big sniff, and his nostrils fill with the unmistakable smell of Hunter shiraz: like damp clay and crushed cloves. There is enough of a demand – just – for O'Shea to continue making wines like this. McWilliam's, the big wine company that bought O'Shea's Mount Pleasant winery in the 1930s, recognise this and let him carry on, even though they make far more money out of fortifieds.

During the 1940s, people like O'Shea, people concerned with making good table wine, were few and far between. But there were enough of them not only to keep the flicker of table wine alive but to continue fanning the flame.

In 1950 the young Penfolds winemaker Max Schubert went to Europe, where exposure to old, great red wines from Bordeaux inspired him to create Grange, Australia's most famous – and arguably most influential – red wine. It's worth remembering, though, that the trip to Bordeaux was a sideline; Schubert was actually on a mission to find out more about sherry production because, at the time, that was Penfolds' core business. Indeed, when Schubert showed his bosses the results of his red wine experiment – massive, concentrated, barrel-fermented shiraz in a totally new style – they were so freaked out that they ordered him to stop making it (he continued in secret and eventually won them round).

Others in the 1950s weren't so narrow minded. This was the decade that saw the Australian wine industry begin to develop its modern image. Entrepreneurial Melbourne wine merchants Sam and David Wynn bought the old cellars in Coonawarra that John Riddoch had established over half a century before and created a brand – complete with adventurous marketing vision – that continues to this day. In the Barossa, Orlando's Colin Gramp revolutionised white winemaking by importing pressure fermentation tanks from Germany – a technique that quickly developed into cool stainless steel fermentation – resulting in delicate, clean rieslings with unprecedented perfume.

Across the country a wave of southern European (mostly Italian) migrants began to challenge the tea-and-Sunday-roast Anglo–Australian way of life. The world came to Australia with the Olympics in 1956, and young Australians promptly began taking themselves and their backpacks to the world. Merchants like winebar owner Jimmy Watson in Melbourne really began travelling to those few old cellars that had survived the fortified years – Wendouree in Clare, Booth's in north-east Victoria – and buying barrels of big red shiraz to bottle and sell across the bar to a new generation of drinkers. The industry began to rumble again.

> When Schubert showed his bosses the results of his red wine experiment – massive, concentrated, barrel-fermented shiraz in a totally new style – they were so freaked out that they ordered him to stop making it (he continued in secret and eventually won them round).

A picnic by the beach. Somebody's brought a screwtop bottle of golden, sweet, gently fizzy Barossa Pearl. Somebody else has brought a dumpy bottle of Kaiser Stuhl rosé and a tall bottle of Ben Ean moselle. And there are a couple of flagons of d'Arenberg's McLaren Vale red hanging around near the barbecue. Nobody's wearing sunscreen. And everybody's smoking.

The 1960s is when the modern wine boom took off. All the brands I've just mentioned (and a whole host more) took table wine out of the dark dinner parties of the few in the know and into the bright sunshine of ordinary people's lives. The big companies (Orlando, Seppelt, Lindemans and the like), funded by the commercial success of these popular wines, began expanding, planting big new vineyards in distant (Coonawarra) and previously untried (Keppoch, later known as Padthaway) places. They also turned their attention to making better red wines for the increasingly discerning market. Emboldened by the boom, they even began a thankfully short-lived push into export markets with wines like Chateau Downunda and Kanga Rouge (no, seriously).

At the other end of the scale, the 1960s also saw the birth of the 'boutique' winemaker. People like Dr Max Lake in the Hunter Valley and Dr Bailey Carrodus in the Yarra Valley started small vineyards with big visions – in much the same way as the nineteenth-century pioneers had. And, in much the same way, their enthusiasm was infectious.

All this boutique activity may have gone unnoticed if it hadn't been for another new 1960s breed, the wine writer. A young Welsh migrant called Len Evans began writing for the *Bulletin* in the early 60s, and, through his columns and work for the Australian Wine Bureau, helped create the thirst for the wines his colleagues were producing. It's hard to imagine one man having so much influence over an industry – over a country's drinking habits – but the industry wasn't the thriving corporate giant it is today – more a collection of mates churning out some great booze.

We're beginning to drift now into the realm of recent memory rather than second-hand reporting. It's easier to imagine Evans, holding court in a Sydney restaurant (as he is still wont to do), raving about the glories of a young Hunter semillon or mature Coonawarra 'claret', partly because Evans and Lake and many of those who drank with them are still very much alive and will tell you their story themselves.

Margaret River, Western Australia, 1973

There's a sticky, grapeskin-stained glass of purple liquid sitting on a white benchtop in the corner of a hastily constructed winery. The winemaker – well, he's a doctor, actually, but because he has planted vines and now made his first wine, he reckons he can give himself this fancy title – is staring at the glass like it's his first newborn child (which it is, kind of). He picks it up and sniffs it. Even though the wine hasn't finished fermenting, he can already smell that wonderful blackcurrant and olive aroma of cabernet sauvignon. It was a risk, planting a relatively unfashionable grape in a completely new region, miles from the closest market. But it looks as though it might have paid off. And before he knows it, he's beaming like a love-sick idiot.

A lot of people spent a lot of the 1970s smiling a lot. A small army of boutique winemakers (and the new wave of medium-sized wineries such as Len Evans' Rothbury Estate in the Hunter Valley) were supported in their endeavours by a wave of technical improvements in the winery, with young, bold whiz-kid consultant winemakers like Brian Croser and Tony Jordan busily running around the country distributing the latest info to have filtered out from the labs (before setting up the now-important wine science course at Charles Sturt University in New South Wales).

Importantly, people like Croser who had studied in California, and Andrew Pirie, who had travelled the world looking for the perfect spot before establishing Pipers Brook Vineyards in northern Tasmania, were keen to develop the Australian wine industry in a global context, to compete with the new wines emanating from California and elsewhere in the New World.

The 1970s saw big chunks of the Australian wine industry pass into (and almost always out of) foreign ownership. Cigarette companies, brewers, pharmaceutical giants all had a go at riding the back of the boom, and almost all of them failed. Wine companies buying other wine companies for their vineyards or equipment or brands had always been a big feature of the industry – Thomas Hardy's 1877 purchase of Dr Kelly's Tintara winery in McLaren Vale, for example, or Seppelt's 1918 purchase of Hans Irvine's

Great Western cellars (which Irvine had in turn bought from its founder, Joseph Best) – but during this decade, the buying and selling had less to do with wine and more to do with cold hard profit.

From a wine drinker's point of view, though, the most important development in the 1970s was the introduction of the wine cask. The silver bladder-in-a-box became an icon of Australian domestic life – up there with Vegemite, the Hill's Hoist and the backyard barbecue, and up there dispensing 'moselle' and 'chablis' from the top shelf in your fridge.

It's easy to poo-poo the cask – on grounds of health, politics and flavour among other things – but there's no doubt that it (and the technological advances that made it possible) built a solid wine drinking culture in this country. Australians each drank about eight litres of wine a year in 1970. By 1985, we were knocking back twenty-one litres, and despite a dip during the recession of the early 1990s, we're still quaffing around twenty. It simply would not have happened without the cask.

Adelaide, South Australia, 1988

The white-coated wine taster picks up the glass of sparkling wine in front of him and gives it a brief swirl before bringing it to his nose. With a deep professional sniff he takes in the aroma – clean, nutty, yeasty, like freshly baked bread – then a sip and a couple of slurpy intakes of breath before the wine is shot out, clinically, into a bucket. Then a brief scribble in pencil on the sheet on his clipboard, and the judge moves on to the next wine. It's so much more fun, he thinks, judging a class of sparkling wine now that people have started using pinot noir and chardonnay from cooler climates, rather than that awful warm climate ondenc and semillon they were using before.

It was also the decade that saw chardonnay shove riesling off the white wine throne.

By the end of the 1980s, 200 years after it all began, the modern industry was really beginning to come together. The various authorities, committees and bodies that sought to control the industry began to be rationalised, and the Label Integrity Programme – an auditing system that guarantees honesty and accuracy in labelling – had been established.

The scale of the inter-winery buyouts grew, culminating in Penfolds buying Lindemans (which included Rouge Homme, Seppelt, Queen Adelaide, etc.) in 1990. The decade also saw some major overseas investment of a nature quite different from the frenzied takeovers of the 70s, such as champagne giant Möet et Chandon's Domaine Chandon venture in the Yarra Valley – resulting in very high quality, internationally styled fizz like the one described above.

All this big business was balanced (in a way) by the increasing number of high-profile winemakers setting up on their own – many leaving comfortable jobs in big companies to do so. This was the decade of Peter Lehmann, of Rocky O'Callaghan at Rockford, Grant Burge and Ian Wilson at Krondorf and Brian Croser at Petaluma, as well as a still-flowing stream of boutiques – doctors and lawyers and pharmacists all keen on the vigneron ideal. It was also the decade that saw chardonnay shove riesling off the white wine throne.

There are some aspects of the 1980s that the industry would perhaps rather forget. The earlier part of the decade, when the white wine boom was still booming, saw a fashion for rather herbaceous, lean, green-tasting cabernet sauvignon. Shiraz was thoroughly out of fashion, so, in the mid-80s when the South Australian government sponsored a vine pull scheme to try and take the pressure off the oversupply of red wine, a fair proportion of old shiraz vineyards were pulled out.

But the late 1980s and early 90s will mostly be remembered, I suspect, for the beginnings of the export revival. The world – particularly that favourite market, the United Kingdom – developed an insatiable thirst for Aussie wine during this period, thanks to some relentless marketing by companies such as Penfolds and Rosemount Estate and individuals such as the Australian Wine Bureau's Hazel Murphy in London who, among other things, arranged to drag plane-loads of British press, trade and buyers around Australia.

I remember working at the International Wine Challenge in London, one of the world's biggest wine competitions, in 1992, and seeing Australian wines win category after category – Coonawarra cabernet triumphing over classed growth Bordeaux, Hunter shiraz coming out on top of turbo Rhone Valley syrah. I remember wandering around the London Wine Trade Fair in the vast hall of Olympia and seeing this almost mad crush around the Australian stands (I remember Don McWilliam keeping his cabernet sauvignon in – shock, horror – an ice bucket, it was so hot, and how natural it seemed for him to be breaking a Golden Wine Rule). And I remember sitting at the back of a tutored comparative tasting of La Chapelle (one of France's great wines) and Penfolds Grange, and listening to the excited murmuring ripple through the room full of pin-striped wine trade veterans as the Granges from the early 1970s and 60s were tasted.

Now all this might seem to be of little interest or relevance to Australian wine drinkers, but you have to remember that without the export boom,

there would be nowhere near as much frantic planting of vineyards or hasty erection of wineries or launching of new labels as there is today. But we'll come to that, we'll come to that.

It wasn't all wine being shipped out of Australia during the late 1980s/early 90s. A growing number of Australian winemakers also began to travel overseas, making wine (usually for British supermarkets) in places as diverse as Moldova, France, Italy and Brazil. The critics would eventually begin to accuse these Flying Winemakers of crafting 'international' soulless wines but, at the time, it revolutionised the wine scene in the UK. It also produced a whole generation of young Australian winemakers who came home with an international perspective and a whole bunch of new ideas about wine styles and quality.

Sydney, New South Wales, 1996

My teeth have been stained a lovely deep purple from all the rich, alcoholic, American-oak aged shiraz I've tasted today. I'm at Wine Australia, '96, the industry's much-hyped showcase exhibition at Darling Harbour in Sydney. Downstairs, hundreds of winemakers are pouring their wares for thousands of eager wine-lovers, but I'm sitting with lots of men and women in business suits in a large auditorium, listening to Len Evans, chairman of Wine Australia, introduce Strategy 2025.

This is a pivotal moment in Australia's recent wine history. The vision outlined in the document is that (deep breath) 'By the year 2025 the Australian wine industry will achieve $4.5 billion in annual sales by being the world's most influential and profitable supplier of branded wines, pioneering wine as a universal first choice lifestyle beverage.' It's just a few words on a piece of paper, but it manages to encapsulate and motivate the industry in the late 1990s.

Since I started writing about wine in 1993 I've spent a disproportionate amount of time, it seems, writing about exports and takeovers and mergers and investment and tax issues – money, money, money, in other words.

The auction market for top Australian wines went crazy during the 90s: more than once I've found myself in a big room full of nervous faces and clicking cameras, watching someone set a new sale record for old bottles of Grange. For a few years after 2025 was announced, a prospectus a week seemed to flop through the letter box announcing some new vineyard scheme or winery float; the fax machine ran hot with press releases announcing some new joint venture between one of Australia's top four companies and a winery in California/Chile/France/Italy; and I spent a huge amount of time being driven around paddocks full of tender young one-year-old vines. And I also watched as fairly bitter disputes over trademarks and regional boundaries raged in and out of the courts.

In other words, the 1990s have seen the wine industry become far more serious than it ever was before. The 1990s have also been a great time to be a lover of Australian wine.

Even though exports and giant increases in sales tax have seen Australia's top wines become rarer and more expensive, this has been offset by the huge investments in new vineyards and new wineries, resulting in unprecedented choice for the consumer. There's nothing like the thrill of coming across a new label and discovering that the wines behind it are fabulous.

As the industry has moved towards defining its wine regions (see the third section of the book for much more on this), it has helped develop a thriving wine (and food) tourism business. And in the cities, a strong economy has resulted in a vibrant and sophisticated restaurant wine scene that is, in many ways, leading the world. Wine is very much a part of the new affluent Australian society. Wine is sexy.

One of the most exciting things for me (bearing in mind what I wrote at the beginning of this chapter) is how the wine industry has rediscovered its heritage. The last few years have seen a succession of anniversaries – 25 years for the boutiques, 100 (even 150) years for the big guys.

It's become de rigueur for the small wineries to throw a bash and pull out some embarrassing pics from the early 1970s of the fledgling winemaker (almost unrecognisable with beard and flares) standing proudly by his basket press, surrounded by wild-looking kids who are now running wineries of their own. It's become equally compulsory for the big companies to commission a book celebrating their achievements, outlining in great and sumptuously illustrated detail the ups and downs of the previous century. It all adds to the depth of the Australian wine experience.

You're standing on a boat in the harbour, surrounded by thousands of people in other boats, all watching the fireworks unfurl in the night sky above you. There's a glass of white wine in your hand, a pinot gris from South Australia, made by one of the newest trendy small producers. Someone passes with a tray of sashimi, and you just can't resist. The cold fish and honeyed, grapey white wine explode in your mouth as the Harbour Bridge explodes in a cascade of light.

In 1970 there were only 160 wineries across Australia. By 1995 that number had risen steadily to about 800. Now, at the beginning of the twenty-first century, that figure has exploded to about 1200. There are well over 120,000 hectares of vines in the ground – almost double the area planted in the late 1980s. And each year these vineyards produce over 1.2 million

tonnes of grapes – twice the amount harvested in 1995. The most sobering facts of all, though, are that cask wine still represents more than half of Australia's wine sales; and that the top twenty companies produce more than ninety per cent of Australia's wine – with the big four (Southcorp, BRL Hardy, Mildara Blass and Orlando Wyndham) accounting for most of that. The momentum that picked up in the 90s shows little sign of slowing down in the noughties (a stupid word but I'm kind of fond of it). The Australian wine industry is positively throbbing with excitement.

New (to Australia) grape varieties like viognier and pinot gris and a whole host of Italian reds are broadening the choice of flavours and wine styles available to the consumer – a very good thing indeed, as people are becoming increasingly willing to try new (usually Asian inspired) foods.

New regions are being pioneered across the country, with adventurous souls trekking out past the existing boundaries and sticking a few vines in the ground. Len Evans' prediction that the best wine region in Australia hasn't even been discovered yet still resonates with possibilities.

In the existing regions, and with the established wineries, quality seems to be improving all the time: as the vines get older and the makers tuck away more experience, we are seeing an ongoing finessing process, resulting in more complex, more satisfying wines. Many winemakers are also rediscovering and making the most of what has been lurking in their backyard for years – neglected grape varieties, vineyards and wines styles are suddenly fashionable once more.

The ever-increasing number of wineries and wines competing for your love has a few in the industry shaking their heads in bemusement. Perhaps the equally strong growth in wine tourism will take up some of the slack. Perhaps developments in on-line retailing will change the whole way we buy wine, and find a new way for these new wineries to get their wines to us.

Look, I can't predict precisely how the industry will develop over the next quarter-century. No one really can. But I am extremely confident that things will probably change dramatically, and they'll change when we're all least expecting it.

Australian Grape Varieties & Wine Styles

Fruit Driven

I began to explore the mysteries of the demon drink in the early 1980s when I was a teenager living in London. To start with, I flirted with it in its northern European form – sweet cider, weak lager and the odd splurge of cheap scotch (a pretty unappetising combination, thinking about it now, but awfully effective at the time).

Then a friend of my parents sent us a mixed case of wine through the Australian Wine Centre, and my tongue went cavorting off in a new direction. In the box there were reds (shiraz, cabernet), and a couple of dry whites … and a wine that really rang my bells. It was, I'm not ashamed to admit, a late harvest muscat.

God, this stuff was good. So luscious, so ripe, like liquid gold. Like sunshine in a glass. It made you happy when you drank it.

Now that I'm almost a grown-up, I'm much more attracted to those shirazes and cabernets than the late harvest wines (at least in public). But I'm still finding plenty of sunshine in my glass.

What seduced me then and seduces me still, of course, is Australian wine's greatest asset: the generous, easy-to-understand, sweet ripe flavour of its fruit – the quality of its grapes.

We've all been sold the idea that the winemaker is the most important part of the winemaking process. We are repeatedly told that Australian winemakers are the most technologically advanced and innovative in the world. This may be true, but I still think the real secret to the quality and success of Australian wine is in the grapes.

And the secret to the grapes is the sunshine. Whether the grapes are grown in the hot irrigated inland areas or up on the side of a cool mountain or down in the chilly volcanic soil of Tasmania, the sunshine is still there.

To get a good grip on Australian wine – to understand its style differences and regional variations – you need to know a little bit about the grapes, especially as the name of the grape variety is usually the biggest word on the label. There are many different types used, and each contributes its own flavours to the finished wine – flavours that can change depending on where and how the grapes are grown, and what happens to them in the winery and the bottle.

I've tried to outline those nuances over the next few pages – and I've given you some food-matching suggestions, too, just so you can work up a nice appetite for lunch. Remember, these food matches are really only suggestions – things that have worked for my palate on a regular basis. They are not golden unbreakable rules, so feel free to ignore them – although how anybody could ignore the thought of a glistening, succulent roast Peking duck partnered with a glass or two of velvety, forest-berry-rich pinot noir I'll never know.

Shiraz

A Barossa grape grower once told me how she felt about her old shiraz vineyard. For her, the gnarled, twisted vines that have been squeezing out great purple wine for over a century are a direct link between the dirt they are anchored and in the people who tend them.

I love this image – that somehow, shiraz is the lifeblood of the ancient Australian soil, and winemakers are the custodians of that relationship. It's emotive stuff, isn't it? The blood of a country. People have fought wars for less.

Shiraz (pronounce it 'shiraarrz' or 'shiraaargh' if you want to sound like a local the next time you're driving through wine country) has been here almost since the beginning. Remember the red wines that amazed those judges in Vienna in 1873? Made from shiraz. The legendary red wines of the 1940s like the Woodley 'Treasure Chest' Coonawarra clarets, and the Great Western burgundies and Maurice O'Shea Hunter reds – shiraz, all of them, or predominantly shiraz. And what about Penfolds Grange, the grandpappy of big Aussie reds? Shiraz, of course. Indeed, until the 1990 vintage was released, it was known as Grange Hermitage – the hermitage bit being a traditional Australian synonym for shiraz, and a nod to the variety's origins on the hill of Hermitage in the northern Rhone Valley in France.

If you drank Australian red wine in the 1990s, then you probably drank more shiraz than anything else. For most of that decade it was far and away the most popular red wine variety – and it shows no sign of slowing down now. Shiraz is the most widely planted grapevine in Australia. There's more of it in the ground even than chardonnay (although chardonnay yields more grapes, so it's the number one variety by volume).

Bearing that in mind, it may surprise you to learn that as recently as the mid-1980s, shiraz grapes were so out of favour with the wine-drinking public that they were being made into shiraz muffins. Honestly. Winemakers were so over the variety that whole vineyards full of it were ripped from the ground. Everybody wanted cabernet instead, and the old workhorse, shiraz, was sent to the vine equivalent of the knacker's yard.

So how did shiraz go from being scorned to being rediscovered and then revered in just over a decade? The answer can be pretty much summed up in one word: export. At about the time when century-old shiraz vines were being ripped up in the Barossa, wine drinkers in the UK and elsewhere were beginning to develop a ferocious thirst for Australian shiraz. The more they clamoured for it, the more we began to realise we may have something special in our own back paddock. Now, we just can't get enough of the stuff.

Shiraz in the vineyard

If you were into making sweeping generalisations, you'd be inclined to lump shiraz into three distinct flavour families, revolving around where the grapes are grown. In the warmest group of regions, shiraz produces the biggest, ripest flavours: big and beefy in the Barossa Valley, more elegance but plenty of oomph in the Eden Valley, sweet and rich in McLaren Vale, powerful but slightly minty in the Clare Valley and central Victoria, dense and heroic in north-east Victoria, earthy in the Goulburn Valley and Mudgee. In the middle ground – Coonawarra, Margaret River, the Grampians – the wines are medium to full, with more elegance but still great intensity. And in the coolest regions – the Yarra Valley, Great Southern, Orange, Canberra, Sunbury – shiraz can be really lean, taut and spicy, often with alarming white-pepper characters.

Oh, and there's one style that sits outside the generalisations. In the Hunter Valley, shiraz has a quite distinct leathery, dusty earth and clove quality that is quite unlike that of anywhere else but can be hauntingly attractive.

Shiraz in the winery

Big, rich, ripe shiraz and sweet, vanilla-scented American oak barrels have a remarkable affinity for each other. It's not surprising, then, that your typical warmer climate Australian shiraz is a combination of the two: the grapes are crushed, fermented furiously (in open vats with the wine frequently pumped over the skins, or in a big rotary fermenting tank), pressed (in an old-fashioned, hand-operated basket press if you're feeling energetic) and then aged in new American oak barrels for a year or so. Often, the wine is pressed off before it has finished fermenting, so that the tail end of fermentation can happen in barrel – resulting in a distinctive, smoky, charry flavour. (A cheaper, if less satisfying, way of approximating this enticing flavour is to chuck big teabags of oak chips into the wine as it ferments in huge stainless steel tanks).

Substituting older or more subtly flavoured French oak barrels for the American barrels is often an option chosen by winemakers in cooler climates, where the fruit flavours are less robust, and you want the end result to be more refined.

Shiraz in the bottle

Few wines can match the richness of ripe black fruit, the heartiness, the sheer Australian-ness of good young shiraz when it's released two years after vintage. Or the stunning, savoury complexity – flavours of caramel, roasting meat, wet clay – and the velvety, entrancing texture of that shiraz after it's spent a decade or so in the cellar. This is the greatness of shiraz: its direct effect on the senses. You don't have to think too hard to enjoy it. You can just sit there and let it work its magic on your tongue.

Shiraz in the belly

Lighter, more peppery, cool-climate shiraz likes to cavort with simple grilled steak, spicy pizza, that kind of thing, while fuller, richer, warmer shiraz loves deep-tasting, heavily sauced roast meat and slow-cooked things. Older shiraz loves game and hard, crumbly cheeses. And mushrooms. With a roaring fire in the open hearth. And with a nice thick rug to roll around on.

Earth Wines

Grenache, Mourvedre (AKA Mataro) and the Pinks

Like shiraz, the red grapes grenache and mourvedre originally came to Australia from the Rhone Valley in France well over 150 years ago. For much of that time, they have been used and abused – planted in the warm and irrigated areas, cropped heavily and turned into fairly ordinary port or bulk red. Some people have recognised the grapes' best qualities over the years – grenache in particular is a crucial component of the finest tawny ports and contributed much to the old South Australian 'burgundies' of the 1950s and 60s – but most winemakers looked upon the pair as useful but uninspiring.

In the last decade, though, as interest in shiraz has intensified, particularly interest in shiraz from older vines, winemakers have also rediscovered their grenache and mourvedre vineyards and started turning them into wine – either single varietals or blended, often with shiraz thrown in for good measure.

Most people lump these new-old-fashioned wines under the heading 'Rhone style'. This may be historically appropriate, but for me it doesn't quite do justice to the wonderful, distinctively Australian flavours the wines can unload onto your tongue – grenache with its riot of spices and raspberries and tobacco, mourvedre with its deep purple fruit and tough tannins.

There's a group of young wine nuts in Adelaide – retailers, waiters, students and just plain nuts – who have come up with a better term. They refer to wines made using grenache, shiraz and mourvedre as 'earth wines' – which may not be original, but I like it. So I'm going to use it too.

The earth wine revival began in the late 1980s, when Barossa winemakers like Charlie Melton and Rocky O'Callaghan realised that the old, low-cropping, half-ignored grenache and mataro vineyards that surrounded them could make pretty smart wine given half the chance. (They also, crucially, realised that if you put 'mourvedre' rather than 'mataro' on the label, it made your wine sound a little more upmarket.)

The revival continued through the early 1990s, when McLaren Vale winemakers such as Chester Osborn at d'Arenberg began paying unprecedented prices for growers' grenache, provided they limited yields to his specifications. And now, as the twenty-first century dawns, the trend looks as though it's here to stay.

A word about alcohol. Grenache (and shiraz) can ripen to extremely high sugar levels, and it is not uncommon to get earth wines of 15 or 16 per cent alcohol. Many people think this is a terrible thing, but I'm not so bothered – as long as there's enough flavour to balance the fire.

Earth wines in the vineyard

It's very much hot country grape growing we're talking about here. Some people persist with grenache and mourvedre in cooler climates but I reckon they're soft in the head. You can kind of get away with cool climate shiraz in a lean, peppery style, but grenache and especially the late-ripening mourvedre really need loads of sun to give them their essential oomph and ripe fruit flavours. This is why warmer regions such as the Barossa Valley and McLaren Vale have done so well with the varieties for over a century. What you really do have to watch out for, though, is the yield. Left to its own devices, a grenache vine will pump out massive amounts of fruit, but to make half decent wine with any kind of concentration, you need to be strict and knock back the tonnage – by hard pruning and even bunch thinning (taking some fruit off the vine before it's ripe so that what's left can ripen properly).

Earth wines in the winery

While the biggest, darkest, most concentrated grenache and mourvedre can be made like a big shiraz – aged in brand-new American oak barrels producing sweet-smelling, raspberry ripple icecream-style wines – many winemakers are moving towards playing down the oak influence and letting the varieties' spicy fruit flavours shine through. Some are beginning to use more subtle, French oak, and a few are rediscovering tradition by ageing their grenaches and blends in big old oak vats. The result is more refined, complex wines. In most cases, too, it pays to blend: while grenache and mourvedre can often taste a little simple on their own (unless they

reds

come from particularly special, old, low-yielding vineyard sites), some of each plus a dollop of shiraz can create a wine that is more than the sum of its parts.

Earth wines in the bottle

Do earth wines age well in the bottle? I'm in two minds about this. Most of the time I like to get stuck into a good grenache or grenache blend when it's young – a year or two after vintage (which is when most are released onto the market), when all its vibrant spice and explosive fruit are still fresh and lively. But then I'll come across an old McLaren Vale 'burgundy' from the late 1960s and be blown away by its deeply plummy fruit, wet clay richness and Vegemitey, savoury edge. Will the new wave wines age as well? There's only one way to find out: start digging that cellar now.

Earth wines in the belly

You can really go a bit wild matching earth wines to food. I'm thinking Moroccan flavours: slow-cooked lamb tagine, cous cous, flat bread dipped in green olive oil and spices. Mushrooms are a must, too – either grilled simply and piled up on sourdough toast, or stewed with wine and herbs (and a few chunks of goat). Whatever you do, though, make sure garlic is involved somehow.

Pink wines

I'm sticking pink wines in here partly because they have nowhere else to go, poor things, and partly because most Australian rosé wines are made from grenache – or at least my favourite ones are. There are two basic ways to make pink wine. You can either press off the wine from a vat of fermenting red grapes before too much colour has been leached from the skins (the best way), or you can add a dash of red to some white (the easiest way). There are two main styles of pink wine produced in Australia: the paler, salmon-coloured wines, often quite dry and more savoury in style (I'm craving spaghetti marinara at this point), and the full-on magenta-coloured, fuller-bodied style, absolutely loaded with ripe berry fruit and often finishing with a touch of sweetness (now I'm back to garlic and outside eating and Mediterranean flavours).

Cabernet Sauvignon...

Right around the world, cabernet sauvignon is held in awe by grape growers, winemakers and wine drinkers alike. It's considered an aristocrat of a vine, upright, sturdy, refined, its long, loose bunches of small, tight berries producing equally stern tannic, austere wines needing years in the bottle to show their best.

Not in Australia. Sure, there are some incredibly tannic, austere wines made, and sure, a few years' slumber in the bottle can produce some mellow flavours in them. But on the whole, Australian cabernet sauvignon is a more approachable and egalitarian creature altogether, especially from the warmer regions.

One of my favourite pastimes is wandering through a barrel hall with a winemaker, tasting young wines, six, nine, twelve months after vintage (I obviously don't have much of a life if this is my idea of wicked fun). And it never ceases to amaze me how drinkable good young cabernet can be: the grape variety is meant to be so unyielding and tannic, especially when young, but this deep purple liquid that the winemaker has just squirted into my glass tastes fantastic – big, yes, powerful, yes, tannic, most certainly, but supple, round ... drinkable.

Likewise, it never ceases to amaze me how wine that is approachable when young can age so well in the bottle. I've drunk twenty- and thirty-year-old Coonawarra cabernets that have stunned me with their liveliness and lingering ripe fruit flavours. Other people have been fortunate enough to taste cabernets produced in the Yarra Valley at the beginning of the twentieth century (lucky bastards) that have, by all accounts, tasted like twenty- or thirty-year-olds. According to popular wisdom, red wine needs to be structured like a tannic packhorse to age well, yet Australian cabernet seems to live for decades by feeding off its fruit as well as its structure.

reds

The relative approachability of good Australian cabernet has a lot to do with its ripeness: in most cases, it's grown in regions that receive enough sunshine to create more mellow tannins and sweeter fruit flavours in the grape skins. Again, this is a sweeping generalisation: a lot of cabernet is still grown in the cooler parts of Australia (Tasmania, southern Victoria, the Adelaide Hills), and can, in less-than-ideal years, produce thin, green, weedy wines. But most – certainly at the cheaper end, are grown in pretty warm spots.

I find that the very best Australian cabernets, the wines with that magical combination of intense berry fruit flavour, fine tannins and savoury, cedary complexity, come from those vineyards that are on the edge – usually with enough sun to get the grapes ripe, but an ever-present threat of the season going cold to keep everybody on their toes.

Cabernet in the vineyard

Another of my favourite pastimes is walking through a cabernet vineyard just before harvest, picking the ripe, juicy bunches and stuffing them in my mouth (I *really* should get out more). The flavour of cabernet grapes is more exciting, I think, than almost any other variety; when you chew on the thick, sweet purple skins you get this explosion of dusty tannins and blackcurrant fruit that gives you such a vivid idea of what the wine's going to taste like.

Cabernet is grown right across Australia, and gives a wide variety of flavours. In the warmer South Australian regions like the Barossa and McLaren Vale, and in central Victoria (Bendigo, the Pyrenees) it can be quite rich, chocolatey, with really ripe black fruits and some dense, sturdy tannins. In the middle (best) ground – my picks would be Coonawarra, Margaret River and the Yarra Valley – it gets this great intensity of black-currant fruit and stunning finesse. And in the cooler areas and years, as I've said, it can lean towards greenness.

Cabernet in the winery

If ripe shiraz and American oak are made for each other, then French oak is the favourite partner of cabernet. This wine's fine tannins, and more intense, elegant fruit seem to prefer the finesse and savoury characters you get in a good French barrel (although the combination of really ripe cabernet and new American oak – especially as a proportion of a blend – can inject some irresistible sweet sexiness into a wine). Despite what I've said about the approachability of Australian cabernet's tannins, there's no doubt that the variety does have them in abundance, so many winemakers try to make them as mellow as possible – by leaving the wine macerating with the skins after fermentation, for example, or leaving it in barrel for longer (up to and exceeding two years).

Cabernet in the bottle

Australian cabernet can and does do well as a single varietal wine, but winemakers are increasingly likely to blend it with other varieties – either to soften the cabernet if it's on the hard side, or to add complexity to the finished drink. There's much more about this on the following pages.

Cabernet in the belly

I'd like to take this opportunity to apologise to all my vegetarian readers for the amount of meat-based food recommendations in this book. But here I go again: I know that it's probably unbalanced and won't get the tick of approval from the Heart Foundation, but I really don't think you can do a good cabernet more of a favour than teaming it up with a full-on retro, all-the-trimmings big hunk of roast beef (cooked rare, of course). *I* go all the way – proper gravy made from the pan scrapings and some nice reduced sticky stock, horseradish cream, Yorkshire pudding, that kind of thing – but *you* don't have to.

reds

...and Friends

Merlot, Cabernet Franc, Malbec, Petit Verdot (and Shiraz again)

There's nothing on this earth stopping any Australian winemaker blending any grape variety with any other grape variety. The winemaker is not even required by law to put the permutation of grape varieties on the label. So, if you wanted to, you could blend some cabernet sauvignon, some shiraz, some zinfandel and even some chardonnay and riesling – if you really wanted to, if you really thought it would make a better wine.

The point is that very few winemakers *do* experiment with this kind of blend. They tend to stick with the accepted combinations. And they stick with the accepted combinations because these tend to work – or have been proven to work time and time again over the centuries.

Cabernet sauvignon's accepted partners are the other so-called 'Bordeaux varieties' (there's that reference to the grapes' French origins again), merlot, cabernet franc, malbec and petit verdot. Even though each of these grapes is also used to make single varietal wine in its own right, I've lumped them together here because they share a kind of family resemblance with, and are often made in a similar way to, cabernet sauvignon (and I've obviously got a deep, dark, desperate need to pigeonhole things under easy headings).

Merlot

Of all the cabernet-friendly grapes, merlot is the most important. It's the one most commonly found blended with cabernet, usually in quite high proportions – often as the dominant partner in the relationship. The reason is simple: merlot ripens earlier than cabernet, and produces wine with rounder fruit flavours and more supple tannin – filling cabernet's famous 'hole' in the middle palate.

These same attributes – ripeness, roundness, suppleness – have helped merlot gain a huge reputation with growers, makers and drinkers alike. It's relatively early days (merlot started appearing in Australian vineyards in any meaningful way only in the 1980s), but already some good wines

reds

have been made. In coolish climates like Coonawarra and the Yarra Valley, merlot has excellent savoury, currant, herbal edges; in the warmer McLaren Vale it can have the most indulgent, smoky, plummy plushness; and in the cooler regions of Western Australia it can produce some extraordinary, intense, concentrated wines.

The concentration and plushness that the variety can display have led many winemakers to ask (and get) some equally plush prices for their wines – inspired by the ludicrous dollars charged by the top merlot-dominant wines from Pomerol in Bordeaux. This is all very well, but I'm far more attracted to Australian merlot's ability to produce extremely attractive, extremely gluggable, reasonably priced red wine in areas such as Langhorne Creek, the Barossa and the King Valley.

I've argued before and I'll argue again that a large quantity of good, low-priced wine available to all does more for the good of humanity than a small quantity of great, high-priced wine available to a select few.

Cabernet Franc

Here's a wasted opportunity. Cabernet franc can, if it's not too influenced by the flavours of an oak barrel, produce some delicious red wines on its own – perfumed, with cherries and small berries, finely tannic, juicy, grippy, and really pleasantly light-bodied. Perfect with simple pizza, pasta, everyday food. The problem is that, in an era of big, alcoholic shiraz and rich, ripe, oaky cabernet, lighter styles of wine are not too sellable (unless they've got a trendy name like pinot noir or sangiovese on the label).

This wasted opportunity is not a great loss, because it means more franc can be used in blends with cabernet sauvignon and merlot, to which it can bring a finesse, a brightness of perfume and a depth of colour, especially when it's from regions like Margaret River and the Yarra Valley.

Malbec

Unlike its more recently adopted cousins, the earthy, dark-coloured, spicy malbec grape has been part of the Australian wine family for ages. It has forged a particularly successful relationship with cabernet sauvignon in the Clare Valley – Clare cabernet malbecs (and shiraz malbecs) display the grape's bramble blackberry fruit very well. Its tendency towards too much earthiness has prevented many winemakers from pursuing it as a single

reds

varietal wine (although a couple have been produced in the Great Southern and Langhorne Creek, and the odd sparkling version has cropped up from time to time), so it usually ends up in cabernet blends – often in proportions small enough not to bother mentioning on the label. I like the variety. I like its brambly earthiness, but I rarely find a wine-maker who'll share my enthusiasm.

Petit Verdot

By contrast, you'll find truckloads of Australian winemakers wildly enthusiastic about petit verdot. This is a very late-ripening variety, which was a problem in its original French home of Bordeaux but is less of a problem in the sunny vineyards of Australia. A couple of very attractive single varietal wines have been made – dark purple fruit and intensity – but most winemakers value it far more in their cabernet blends. It seems to add an, oh I don't know, an extra layer of complexity, depth and length of flavour. You'll see it crop up far more in Australian wines in the future.

(And shiraz again)

This is not a mistake. I know we've already looked at shiraz as a star in its own right and as a member of the earth wine ensemble. But it also has a long tradition in Australia of being blended with cabernet.

Merlot *et al* are only recent arrivals in this country, so for most of our wine history warm and friendly shiraz has been used to comfort cabernet in its sterner moments. This may have been a marriage of convenience – and one that may have gone against accepted wisdom – but it turned out to be a most delicious coupling. Shiraz's rich round fruit seems to fit so snugly into cabernet's outstretched and welcoming arms.

The arrival of merlot *et al*, the trendiness of pinot noir and Italian varietals, and the renaissance of the earth wines have taken the spotlight away from this traditional Aussie blend a bit, certainly at the higher-profile, premium end of the market. But I suspect it may be due for a bit of a comeback, as it really is a combination that we know works extremely well – and one that is uniquely Australian. After all, many of our great wines of the 1950s and 60s were shiraz cabernets (or cabernet shirazes), and when the export boom took off in the 80s, it was (and is) a cheap shiraz cabernet, Jacob's Creek, that led the way in the UK.

Pinot Noir

You know, I'd have to check, but I don't think I've got a single bottle of Australian pinot noir in the house. Not one. I buy them. I stick them away in the badly insulated cupboard I laughingly think of as my cellar. I even get sent them for free by various winemakers hoping for a review. But I just can't seem to hold on to them.

More often than not, I'm cooking dinner and I think to myself, now what do I want to drink? And before you know it I've whipped the cork out of that bottle of pinot I'd been saving for a special occasion. Or I get two different bottles through the post and immediately think Ah, let's do a comparative tasting!

Now this either means I'm a hopeless alcoholic, or it means I'm rather fond of pinot noir. I like to think it's the latter, and I rather like to think that I'm not alone: Australian pinot noir is still terribly fashionable, even after well over ten years of hype and hoopla. Not surprisingly, either, because it's a bloody great wine to just sit there and drink – not as big as a cabernet, not as alcoholic as a shiraz, but just right, with light to medium-bodied, alluring, soft fruit and heaps of character.

Although pinot has been hip for a decade or so, it's been grown in Australia since the very beginning. From the Hunter Valley to Tasmania, your average early settler–vigneron would almost undoubtedly have chucked a few pinot noir sticks in the ground and made a passable red wine out of it (and probably called it 'burgundy' in a reference to where the vine originally … you've got the picture by now). That pinot got hip at all is thanks to two developments – the rush to make wine in cooler climates in the 1970s (pinot really needs a long, cool ripening season to show its best); and the growth of the premium sparkling wine market: it is, with chardonnay, one of the best grapes for making good bubbly with.

When the first of the new-wave pinots started appearing in the late 1970s and early 80s a lot of people got very excited because the wines often had a passing resemblance to red burgundy, from France. As the winemakers have experimented more, though, trying out new clones of the

reds

vine, trying new tricks in the winery and, more importantly, watching as their vines matured (producing more concentrated flavours) the wines have begun to show more distinctly Australian, and distinctly regional, flavours and styles. I think Australian pinot noir has improved dramatically over the last few years – and will get better and better.

Pinot in the vineyard

Pinot noir can be terribly fussy about where it's grown. Even in the same region, it might perform well on one hill and not so well on the other – even better in the middle of the hill compared to the bottom or the top. This is true of other varieties, too, but not quite so marked as it is in pinot. So even though it's possible to make generalisations about which regions do best with pinot – southern Victoria (Yarra Valley, Mornington Peninsula, Gippsland, and so on), the Adelaide Hills, Tasmania – within those regions there can be a spread of quality. One of the biggest variables is the vine age and cropping level: again, these two factors affect all varieties, but they seem to express themselves more vividly in pinot – as in, the older the vine and lower the crop, the better the wine (there I go again, generalising sweepingly).

Pinot in the winery

Making pinot noir allows winemakers to really immerse themselves in the romance of winemaking. For a start, many winemakers are playing with spontaneous fermentation: rather than add a cultured yeast to the crushed grapes (normal Aussie winemaking practice), they will wait for the wild (or naturally occurring) yeasts to start fermentation (they claim it makes a more complex wine). Most pinot makers are also big fans of '*pigeage*' or plunging the cap of skins down into the fermenting wine – which, if you're really gripped by the winemaking bug, means getting your gear off and jumping into the vat.

Since the mid 1990s, it's also become very common for pinot makers to cold-macerate their crushed grapes before fermentation begins (which means just letting them sit in a big tank doing nothing) – giving more colour and bigger fruit flavours.

Pinot in the bottle

Pinot noir fermented in stainless steel is often released as early as six months after vintage – and dangerously gluggable, strawberry fruity stuff it can be, too. Pinot noir aged in barrel (almost always French oak) tends to be released a year or so after vintage, and while it's usually ready to drink there and then, the best examples can develop in the bottle for five, ten, twenty years, picking up delicious wet undergrowth complexity as the wine ages (and it is delicious, I swear). Just because it's not built like a wharf labourer doesn't mean it won't age well.

Pinot in the belly

As I think I may have said, pinot noir is one of my favourite food wines, and one of my favourite pinot foods is duck (and I'm definitely not alone here). Duck roasted with honey and coriander, classic Peking duck, duck casserole, duck sausage, duck terrine – I don't care, as long it's duck and the wine in my glass is pinot. Guinea fowl's good, too, as is quail. And squab. Oh, and crispy-skin salmon steaks, or tuna, or trout, surprisingly enough.

It's worth making mention of three other red grapes that share some characteristics with pinot. The first is gamay, the grape responsible for beaujolais in France, and planted in Australia in only one or two spots – which is a shame, I think, as it can produce quite charmingly delicious, cherry–fruity, light-to-medium-bodied, drink-now-with-bistro-food wine. The second is pinot meunier, usually a grape used for sparkling wine (see elsewhere for more) but a couple of vineyards turn it into an earthier, chewier version of pinot noir. The third, tarrango, I'm only including for completeness' sake: it's a grape variety specially developed for Australian conditions and only really marketed by one company (Brown Brothers), and it's usually a bit like gamay without the charm.

reds

Club Med

The Italians and the Spanish

The grape varieties featured in this section occupy such a tiny fraction of vineyard land in Australia that you'd have to ask why I'm even bothering. The answer is that they represent some major shifts in both the industry and the market – the search for new and exciting flavours, for example, and the search for wines that are good with food, and the search for grape varieties that are suited to Australia's soils and climate. In other words, they offer a glimpse of the future of Australian wine – or one part of it, at least.

Italian migrants have played a big role in developing twentieth-century Australian society. They have been coming since the beginning of the country's white history, attracted to the goldfields, then, after the Second World War, attracted by the idea of starting a new life in a big new land. They have established significant communities in both urban and rural areas and have had a profound effect on Australia's attitudes towards food and drink.

It was only a matter of time, then, until one or two enterprising grape growers and winemakers would look up from their bowls of pasta one day and ask themselves why Australia's wine grapes were mostly the 'classic' French varieties. What about the thousands of grape varieties across Italy? Or the rest of the world, for that matter? Surely there's got to be some obscure grape out there that makes wine every bit as good as – maybe even better than – chardonnay, cabernet and riesling? Hey, why don't we find out?

So in the last fifteen years, that's precisely what people have been doing. I spent a lot of time in the late 1990s going to tastings of Australian wines made from Italian grapes, or attending seminars about their potential – I even helped judge the inaugural Australian Sangiovese Challenge, for God's sake (I thought twelve entries was pretty good going for a first effort). The next country ripe for exploration is Spain, whose indigenous red grapes may be even better suited to Australian conditions.

Sangiovese

The red grape leading the Italian charge. It's the main grape responsible for Tuscany's famous red wine, chianti, and early attempts in Australia have been pretty encouraging, especially from warmer areas like McLaren Vale and the Clare Valley: the wines do a good job of displaying the variety's sour cherry fruit and grippy tannins – and are great drinking with food like pizza and pasta.

What growers have come to realise, though, is that the sangiovese they've been working with up to now is not a great clone, so new, better clones of the vine have been imported from Italy and are being planted – which means we should see even better wines in the future. What winemakers have come to realise is that a better wine is often made when sangiovese has ten per cent of something else blended in – cabernet, for example. Also, like pinot noir, sangiovese makes only a pleasant wine if cropped too high, but has the potential to be great if cropped low.

Nebbiolo

The red grape many *would like* to see leading the Italian charge. It comes from Italy's north west, and makes the famously tannic, burly wines of Barolo and Barbaresco. In Australia, the best wines made from it so far (and they are few) have possibly done nebbiolo no favours: they are too varietally correct, too tannic, too brutal, too different. Nebbiolo is perhaps too far out of the Australian drinker's experience to ever achieve anything more than niche notoriety. But that suits nebbiolo-lovers like me, because it means there'll be more of them to go around.

Barbera

The red grape that many suspect *will eventually* lead the Italian charge. This north-west Italian variety may not have the glorious role models of Chianti or Barolo to inspire growers and winemakers to heights of passion, but it has lovely, round, ripe, plummy fruit. And fruit, as I keep telling you, is what makes Australian wines so popular. It has, so far, made some very attractive, very approachable wines. It could be the Italian grape that introduces Australian drinkers to the genre – and inspires them to move on to nebbiolo and sangiovese.

reds

Dolcetto

The red grape that will *never* lead the Italian charge. In Italy, this can be really lovely stuff – vibrant, lively, light and quaffable – but here it's a pleasant wine at best, without the verve of its Italian model. Again, it's early days, but few are likely to persist as it's a notoriously temperamental vine to grow.

And this is just scratching the surface. There are other Italian varieties that have been grown in Australia for years but whose potential has never been realised. Brown Brothers, for example, have been putting a red grape called mondeuse into a blend with shiraz and cabernet for decades – which shows how ahead of their time they were, because mondeuse is another name for the Italian variety, refosco. One grower in the Macedon Ranges has done some really interesting things with lagrein, a cool-climate red grape from the north east of Italy, and there are high hopes for the southern Italian varieties such as aglianico and nero d'avola, particularly in Australia's warmer regions.

It's all go. Watch, as they say, this space.

Tempranillo

If Italy was the flavour of the decade with grape growers in the 1990s, then Spain may well be the flavour of the decade in the 00s. At least I hope it will, because I love the Spanish variety tempranillo and rather fancy the idea of planting a vineyard of it myself – and I'm going to look like a right goose if I'm the only one doing it (then again, I'll have cornered the market ...).

Seriously, the great red grape of Spain is beginning to cause a stir among grape growers in Australia, and there are some tentative vineyards being planted. The attraction is tempranillo's ability to produce really soft, fruity, drink-now red wine in warmer climates, and really serious, dark, age-worthy wine in cooler climates – especially if blended with other grapes for complexity. Its suitability is reinforced when you consider that tempranillo's traditional Spanish blending partners grenache and graciano have been grown here for over a century (graciano, like grenache, was used for port production, but as a table wine adds useful acidity to tempranillo's softness).

Again, this is one to watch.

Deep Purple

And then there's the rest of the mob. The unusual, exotic, useful and just plain dull red grapes that don't fit conveniently under any one banner. Again, these grapes are not produced in any great quantity – or if they are, you probably don't get to read about it on the outside of the four litre cask.

Zinfandel

Like tempranillo, a big personal favourite but, unlike tempranillo, a grape that has been grown here for a few decades. Until recently, zinfandel was planted only in very isolated spots scattered right across the country – in Western Australia, Clare, McLaren Vale, Mudgee – literally the sole passion of single winemakers, rather than any kind of regional trend. These are all warm climates, and the late-ripening zin occasionally turned in a blinding performance, producing (as it does from the best Californian vineyards) huge wines with enormous spicy, funky, earthy bramble character – wines so good, in fact, that they made you wonder why more people weren't playing with the variety.

In the last five years, new zin plantings in cooler spots – the Adelaide Hills, King Valley, Eden Valley – have produced some lovely, more elegant but no-less-spicy wines. But still it refuses to take off. Perhaps it's too similar to shiraz (which can do a good job of huge and spicy itself), or perhaps its more temperamental character in the vineyard has put people off. Whatever, I just wish there was more of it about.

Durif

The winemakers of Rutherglen have adopted this as a regional speciality, even though it is grown elsewhere (albeit in tiny amounts). It suits that region's big, brutish style, as well: it can make massively dense, earthy, tannic wines with enormous weight and depth that evolve slowly in the bottle for years and years. Very useful if you want to give a pinot noir drinker nightmares.

reds

Chambourcin

A hybrid variety (meaning it is a cross between two or more other varieties) that has been particularly successful with growers in warm, humid climates such as coastal New South Wales, thanks to its good mildew resistance. Like many hybrids, it has almost unnaturally bold, purple colour, really assertive purple berry fruit and not much complexity. It can make a good pizza wine for early drinking, but seldom heaves itself above that into the realm of greatness.

Ruby Cabernet

Another hybrid vine and again valued mostly for its ability to produce lots of highly coloured grapes (a dash of ruby cabernet does wonders for an insipid-looking shiraz, for example). Again, pleasant is the word that springs to mind when tasting even the best straight ruby cabernets. Not to be confused with rubired, an even less inspiring hybrid with red skin and red flesh but almost no flavour.

There are also historic plantings of other grapes that have fallen out of fashion such as cinsaut, which survives in Rutherglen (where it's rather romantically called Blue Imperial), and Great Western (where it's even more evocatively known as Black Prince). And there are increasing plantings of Portuguese red grapes used for fortified wine production – but more of them later.

reds

Chardonnay

I feel just a little bit naughty admitting this to you, but I still love chardonnay. I do.

According to the style gurus, Australian chardonnay is meant to be old hat. We're all meant to be bored with it, apparently, fed up with its easy, fruit salad and vanilla oak charms, eager to pin our hopes on the new and trendy white wines like viognier.

Well I'm sorry, but I'm not bored. And neither are most of the wine drinkers out there in the real world. Just look at the figures. There are more chardonnay grapes picked across Australia each year than any other grape variety. Chardonnay is far and away the most-sold grape variety in wine shops across the country. And they're still crazy for it in London and San Francisco.

Not bad going for a grape variety that didn't register on Australia's official statistics thirty years ago. Small pockets of it had been grown here for years – since Busby's time in the early nineteenth century – but for some inexplicable reason, the great white grape of Burgundy didn't take off until the 1970s.

Veteran Hunter Valley winemaker Murray Tyrrell tells a great story of jumping the fence of an old Penfolds vineyard in the late 1960s and stealing chardonnay vine clippings to experiment with – experiments that turned into Australia's first commercial chardonnay, Tyrrell's Vat 47, a couple of years later. This may or may not be true (others, such as Craigmoor in Mudgee, claim equal credit for launching chardonnay onto an unsuspecting public around this time) but it doesn't matter: by the beginning of the 1980s, chardonnay was absolutely the In Thing.

To start with, Australia's early chardonnays were quite clumsy wines – golden-coloured, unsubtle, richly fruity, with loads of sweet oak flavour from time spent in barrel. But as the years passed and people learned more about the best places to plant the grape and the best ways to handle it in the winery, the style was refined.

whites

As the twenty-first century begins, I see three distinct tiers of chardonnay in Australia. At the bottom, broad base of the pyramid there is a sea of reliable, well-made peachy wine, usually with a dash of oak flavour adding interest and usually at an attractively low price. Then you have a lake of medium-priced wines, often with a little more depth of flavour and oak influence but sometimes with a predictable sameness of character (I do admit I'm bored of these). And then, at the top, you find a babbling stream of exceptional wines, often from single, mature vineyards, that manage to convey a sense of place and style as well as being bloody good drinks.

Chardonnay in the vineyard

Chardonnay is incredibly eager to please. Stick a chardonnay vine in the ground almost anywhere in the country – no, absolutely anywhere in the country – and the thing will grow, produce ripe fruit and make you happy. Stick a chardonnay vine in the ground in those areas that the variety has a particular affinity for, however, and it can produce grapes that produce great dry white wine with complexity and satisfaction.

Chardonnay can show diverse and distinct regional differences, depending on where in Australia it's grown. In the warm Hunter Valley you can get wines whose honeyed pineapple flavours ooze all over your tastebuds. In the cooler regions like the Adelaide Hills and Orange you get much more delicate, intense, white-peach-perfumed wines. In southern Victoria – Yarra Valley, Mornington Peninsula, Geelong – and Tasmania the wines can be crisp, citrussy, fine. And in Margaret River you can get wines of incredible concentration and finesse. Of all the white grapes, chardonnay usually produces wines with the fullest body and highest alcohol – 13, 14 even 14.5 per cent are not uncommon.

Chardonnay in the winery

Even though they've had only a quarter century to play with chardonnay, Australian winemakers have tried almost every conceivable trick in the book with the variety. They have fermented it in barrels and then aged it in barrels to produce a savoury, toasty, complex style of wine. They have put it through malolactic fermentation (the bacterial conversion of the wine's hard malic acid to softer, lactic acid) to augment the variety's naturally round, rich texture and flavour. They have kept the wine in contact with its lees (the dead yeast cells and bits of pulp that settle on the bottom of the barrel) to increase complexity. And they have cold-fermented it in stainless steel tanks to produce a light, fruity, crisp wine (for a while during the 1990s 'unwooded chardonnay' was all the rage). Chardonnay is also one of the best varieties for making into sparkling wine – but you'll read all about that a few pages further on.

Chardonnay in the bottle

Some people are adamant that Australian chardonnay should be drunk as soon as it's released onto the market – which is usually six months after vintage for cheaper and unwooded styles and nine months to a year or so after vintage for the more serious, wood-matured versions. On the whole, I'd tend to agree, but there's no doubt that some (usually the more expensive ones, from the cooler climates) do improve with age. Even two or three years stashed a away in a cool dark place can add depth and complexity to a good, medium-priced Aussie chardonnay.

Chardonnay in the belly

Again, familiarity has possibly bred a touch of contempt as far as chardonnay and food go. People are so busy espousing 'modern' marriages like riesling and Thai cuisine (as I am about to overleaf) that they forget what a great food wine chardonnay can be. Mouth-wateringly good combos that I've come across over the years include rich and complex chardonnay with barbecued lobster (only relevant if you're prepared to really splash out); lighter-bodied chardonnay with scallops and lighter shellfish; creamy, malolactic-influenced chardonnay with runny white mould cheeses; and even full-bodied chardonnay with red meat. Garlic-stuffed roast chicken is great, too. In fact, the only thing I'd be wary of is trying to match heavily oaked chardonnay with spicy Asian dishes: oak and chilli can be rather cantankerous palate partners.

Riesling

When chardonnay stormed onto the Australian wine scene in the 1970s and 80s, veteran wine drinkers must have felt like they were witnessing a bloody military coup. For decades, riesling had sat unchallenged as the king of the country's white wines. The noble grape had first established a foothold when German settlers came to South Australia in the 1840s, and during the twentieth century it had been responsible for some legendary wines.

Here, now, was this upstart chardonnay grape, strutting its blowzy, peachy, oaky obviousness all over the place, seducing everybody from the connoisseurs to the common person on the Coogee omnibus. The wine veterans probably hoped it was just a passing fad. They probably predicted (not very confidently) that riesling's day would come again.

They were wrong on one count: chardonnay obviously wasn't a passing fad. But they could have put money on riesling, because it didn't take the challenge lying down. A decade or two down the track, top quality Australian riesling has begun to edge back into wine drinkers' good books, especially recently. Indeed, thanks to the rise of chardonnay leading to many old riesling vineyards being grubbed out, demand for the very best rieslings exceeds supply.

And a good thing, too. Australia is second only to Germany in the quality of its best rieslings (I'm going to get letters from winemakers in Alsace and New Zealand and Austria about this, but I don't care – it's one of very few things that I feel strongly jingoistic about). It was about time we started appreciating them again.

The great thing about good Australian riesling is that it combines all of the variety's charms – perfume, zest, complexity – with a dryness that makes it perfect for drinking with food. The other great thing about Australian riesling is that it's usually exceptional value for money – even though it's certainly popular again, it's not so popular that winemakers can get away with inflating the prices too much (like they're doing with many insanely sought-after, ultra-premium shirazes). After all, riesling doesn't need expensive new oak barrels.

Just a quick note about the name. Accurate labelling was not a priority for much of Australia's winemaking history, and the name 'riesling' was chucked around with gay abandon. So semillon was known as 'Hunter riesling' and casks of sweet white were labelled 'riesling'. To counter this, producers of *real* riesling labelled their wine Rhine riesling – which, confusingly, made you think it was from Germany, rather than the vineyard down the road.

Now don't worry too much about this, because I'm glad to say that after much wringing of hands and arguing, the industry has decided to stop the misleading labelling. From 2001, all wine called riesling has to be precisely that: the real thing. Which can only help the cause.

Riesling in the vineyard

Because riesling has been around for so long in Australia, it has had a chance to establish a strong hierarchy of regions. Right up at the top of the tree are the Clare Valley and the Eden Valley, both in South Australia, the first famous for its full-flavoured, lime-juicy examples of the grape, the second for its austere, steely, long-lived versions. Immediately below these two areas on the traditional pecking order is the warmer Barossa Valley, which produces rounder flavours, followed by Coonawarra, which is better known for its cabernet but can turn out lovely, flavoursome riesling. In the last thirty years, other regions have claimed a spot on the ladder (and that's the last time I mix my metaphors). Western and central Victoria is home to a few really perfumed examples, and Tasmanian rieslings can be hauntingly delicate, crisp and fine. But the region that has really shone is Great Southern, in Western Australia, with wines of great complexity and longevity. What these regions all have in common (apart from the Barossa Valley) is good cool autumns, resulting in wines with plenty of clean, juicy acidity.

Riesling in the winery

With riesling, it pays to keep it simple. All you need to make great wine is already there in the grape – zesty acidity, delicate aromas, vibrant flavour. The last thing you want to do is stuff that up by mucking around with things too much. So most Australian riesling is made in a similar way: the grapes are crushed and pressed and fermented cold, in stainless steel, to capture all the subtleties. It is usually fermented to dryness (meaning all the sugar is converted to alcohol), but often there may be a little residual sugar left in the wine, giving it approach-ability and softness. Sometimes, enzymes are added during fermentation to increase the aroma, although this is becoming less common.

Riesling in the bottle

Almost all Australian riesling is bottled soon after fermentation (within a few months) to retain its fresh-ness. This is one of the two times that it will be at its best – when it's still bursting with the nervous energy of the grapes on the vine. The second time to drink Aussie riesling is after it's had some time to age in bottle – five years, say, or ten – where it can transform into a quite different, golden, honeyed wine. At the moment, I'm dead keen on drinking my rieslings young – I love all the fruit and zest and verve. But occasionally a mature bottle will make my hair curl with its complex smells (like coffee grounds and white toast and lime marmalade) and incredible intensity.

Riesling in the belly

I admit to having a one-track mind when it comes to matching Australian riesling with food. Sure, I've enjoyed old examples with pheasant and young examples with oysters, but I'm far more likely to be thinking Chinese, Thai and Japanese when the riesling corks start popping. Rice paper rolls stuffed with fat prawns; delicate white fish fillets steamed with lemon grass and chilli; spicy salt calamari; those incredible garlic chive dumplings you get at Yum Cha on a Sunday – this is riesling food for me.

Semillon

When Australia finally becomes a Republic – and I'm not holding my breath, here – the wine we toast the new president with should be a semillon. Unfurl the new flag, bung on the new anthem, and let's start uncorking some bottles of Australia's icon wine. After all, there are few wine styles that we can truly claim as our own, as uniquely Australian, but semillon – traditional semillon, from the Hunter Valley – is one of them.

Australian chardonnay, riesling, cabernet – the best examples of these wines sit comfortably among the world's best examples because, stylistically, there are many similarities. Traditional Aussie semillon at its best isn't all that similar to anything – but it's a delicious drink.

The problem is, it can be so different in relation to more modern mainstream wine styles that it can be hard to convince people how good it is. I teach a lot of introductory wine courses, and I always try to squeeze in a couple of Hunter semillons – one very young example, with its clean, rather neutral-tasting freshness, and one bottle-aged example, with its remarkable glowing gold colour and aromas of hot buttered toast.

Even when the older wine is a really great bottle, I watch the faces around the table struggling to come to grips with the wine in their mouths. It smells oaky and rich (even though it's never so much as sneezed at an oak barrel), but it tastes dry and kind of lean at the finish (thanks to the relatively low 10 or 11 per cent alcohol). It's not an easy style to understand, but it's worth persisting with.

I have a theory about how the traditional style came about. The Hunter Valley is notoriously wet at vintage time – the heavens can often open just before the grapes are ready to be picked. Semillon is a very thin-skinned grape, and susceptible to mould and rot when it's damp (more about why this is not always a bad thing later in the book).

So some bright spark decides some time in the 1800s to pick the semillon early, before the rain, when the grapes aren't perhaps as ripe as they could be. The wine he produces turns out to be light, green, even a little thin, thanks to its low alcohol. In fact, our innovator doesn't like it all that much, so he stuffs it away in a dark corner and promptly forgets about it.

Then, five years later, he stumbles across the wine again, and, just for the hell of it, opens a bottle. The transformation into a complex, golden nectar floors him. He runs out to tell all his mates: 'Guys! Guys! You'll never guess …' and a classic wine style is born.

There's more to Australian semillon than this classic style. In South Australian regions like the Barossa and Clare Valleys, for example, you're more likely to find semillon aged in oak, like chardonnay. There are still plenty of budget blends of semillon and chardonnay being produced in the big vineyard regions like the Riverland; it's another uniquely Australian style that has won many friends around the world with its ripe sunny flavours. And semillon also finds its way into cheap bubbly and expensive botrytis-affected dessert wines (as I say, there's more on this elsewhere).

But the traditional Hunter style is the one I'll be drinking on Independence Day.

Semillon in the vineyard

Semillon's heartland is the Hunter Valley. But it is grown right across the country, producing a range of different fruit flavours. In Mudgee, only a

whites

couple of hours' drive from the Hunter, the flavours are similar, if a little riper and rounder. In the Barossa and Clare Valleys in South Australia, it's riper again, with a distinct lemon tang running through it. And in the cool Adelaide Hills, Yarra Valley and Margaret River it can be totally different – green beany and really crisp. It's in these last three regions that you'll often find it blended with sauvignon blanc (see the next page for more on this).

Semillon in the winery

The two main techniques for making Australian semillon couldn't be more diametrically opposed. On the one hand you have the trad (Hunter) style where the grapes are picked green, fermented cold in a stainless steel tank (it used to be big old wooden or concrete vats in the bad old days) and bottled early – preferably then to be cellared for years before release. On the other hand you have the 'modern' (South Australian) style which treats semillon in a similar fashion to chardonnay – picking riper, barrel ageing, bottling later but always releasing it when young.

Semillon in the bottle

I used to think it was only the trad Hunter-style semillon that you could drink twice – once when it's young, then again when it's been developing in bottle. More exposure to older bottles of the 'modern' style, though, has convinced me that these can age well, too, changing from lemon-and-toasty, fresh things to really complex, deep, hedonistic drinks.

Semillon in the belly

But what to drink it with? You've probably got the picture by now that there are many faces of semillon. Well there are as many options when it comes to food. Young unwooded semillon particularly likes plain fresh seafood; young wooded semillon needs something slightly more robust – chicken cooked with olives and fennel, say. Older semillon of any complexion is more adventurous – it can handle Asian-influenced dishes, particularly those involving grilled or fried fish, and it's surprisingly good with mild piggy dishes – penne tossed with a ragu of pork, white wine and cream, say, with lemon zest thrown in for good measure.

whites

Sauvignon Blanc & Sauvignon Blends

Australians are, on the whole, not terribly good losers. Take the Olympics. Unless you can win a gold medal and break the world record and be good in front of the camera then sorry, buddy, but neither the TV commentators nor the public at large will want to know you.

But when it comes to sauvignon blanc, I think most Australian winemakers are quite prepared to admit that the New Zealanders are up there on the podium, showing off the gold. There is no wine region in Australia that can match the combination of pebbly soils and cool sunlight in places like Marlborough, in New Zealand's south island. And as it's the unique soils and climate that produce that region's pungent intensity of gooseberry fruit flavour, we realise we can't quite do what they do.

Not that this stops us trying. Sauvignon blanc is planted right across Australia, from the warmest to the coolest regions, and makes a wide variety of styles – most of them very good in their own right. The Adelaide Hills has claimed it as a regional speciality, and with good reason: of all Australia's examples, good sav blanc from the Adelaide Hills is probably closest in style to the pungent whack of flavour you get in a good Marlborough wine.

Many 'serious' wine critics talk the variety down because of its immediately recognisable and easy-to-understand flavours – it's nice, they say, I suppose, but you couldn't possibly drink more than one glass, darling – but wine drinkers are quite happy to ignore the experts and keep quaffing.

Australia may have let the Kiwis win with varietal sauvignon blanc, but it has claimed the sauvignon blend for its own – especially the sauvignon–semillon blend. Sauvignon blanc and semillon are natural partners: the green tang of the sav blanc melding beautifully with the lemon roundness of the semillon. In some cases, a third, richer-tasting variety, muscadelle, is added to the blend in tiny amounts to add even more complexity (you'll read more about muscadelle in the section on fortified wines).

Sauvignon in the vineyard

If you grow sav blanc in too warm a climate, the flavours you end up with in the bottle can be quite ripe, round, tropical – like paw paw or melon. There's quite a bit of this style made in Australia – in the Riverland and Sunraysia, even in the warmer parts of McLaren Vale. Personally, I much prefer sav blanc that's been grown in the cooler regions – the Adelaide Hills, say, or Orange in central New South Wales, or Tasmania – because it produces wines with much more crisp, zesty, passionfruity zing. As for the sauvignon–semillon blends, while Margaret River and the Yarra Valley seem to be leading the field, the combo crops up elsewhere in the country.

Sauvignon in the winery

While most sav blanc is made in a clean, unwooded style – fermented cold in stainless steel and bottled young – many winemakers are coming to the conclusion that blending in a small proportion of barrel-fermented sav blanc can help bring depth and complexity to the wine. Sauvignon–semillon blends come in two distinct styles: really fresh and pungent unwooded wines, and much more serious, nutty, textured wines fermented and aged in barrel.

Sauvignon in the bottle

The accepted wisdom is that sav blanc doesn't age well in the bottle; that it should be drunk as young as possible – within twelve months of vintage – to make the most of its vivacious, zesty personality. But there are exceptions, such as the better oak-aged sauvignon–semillon blends, which can develop nicely in bottle, turning into great fish wines after five or so years.

Sauvignon in the belly

Sav blanc is one of the best food wines – at least with the kind of food that I like eating. Try finding the freshest raw vegies you can get your hands on – crisp baby carrots, snow peas, green beans – dip them into young, fruity extra virgin olive oil, then into good sea salt, then pop them in your mouth, then take a sip of sauvignon. Or make a salad with rocket and pillowy-fresh goats cheese and be stunned by how well it goes with sav blanc. For sauvignon–semillon blends, try a salad nicoise (heavy on the anchovies) or pan-fried scallops.

whites

My Own Sweet Gewurztraminer

whites

I once visited a winery which had the most fantastic explosion of roses in the car park. One bush in particular was laden with big, heavy blooms – really extravagant dusty pink flowers that were begging to be smelled. So I did: I bent down and stuck my schnoz right into the soft, satiny petals – and was overcome by the most extraordinary smell of gewurztraminer.

Not just any old gewurz, either, but one particular wine – a luscious, bottle-aged gewurz I drank once that came from an old (now defunct) vineyard in the Barossa Valley, with hedonistic, exotic aromas of lychees and perfume, and – well, roses. So I picked the bloom and carried it with me in the car for the rest of the day, sniffing it every now and then, and marvelling at how, the more it decayed, the more uncannily like gewurz it smelled.

I am a big fan of the gewurztraminer grape, and I think Australia is a great place to grow it. I love the best wines that are produced here – I think that they are some of the best food wines you can find. The bad news is that I am in a tiny minority: the bright sun of fashion has gone down on serious Australian gewurz, and hardly anybody appreciates it any more. Which means hardly anybody is making it seriously any more. But the good news is that this is my wine book and I'll cry if I want to – so you're getting a discourse on gewurz here that's out of all proportion to its popularity.

In some ways, gewurz's unmistakable sweet flavour was its own undoing. Even though it produced some lovely wines in the Barossa and Clare, and was highly regarded (well, relatively highly regarded), when the white wine boom of the 1970s came along, it was press-ganged into teaming up with riesling in cheap, sweet blends called traminer rieslings.

A few hardy winemakers have persisted – Knappstein in the Clare Valley, Pipers Brook in Tasmania, Delatite in high-country Victoria, Chatsfield in the Great Southern and others. And what they all have in common is that they make their gewurz in a dry style – ripe, fat, spicy, lychee-packed, but dry. Like riesling, gewurz is best made as simply as possible – cold fermentation, early bottling – to stop the riot of aromatics escaping.

As I say, these top gewurzes are food wines. Think of the suggestions I made for riesling and turn up the volume a notch or two. Extravagantly spiced, slow-cooked Thai curries; the more adventurous Malaysian offal dishes; Middle eastern aromatic cous cous extravaganzas (the rose water, the harissa, the gewurz, the marriage in the mouth – *ahhhh*); even pungent washed rind cheeses. You can really let the imagination run riot.

whites

Home Away From Rhone

Marsanne, Roussanne, Viognier

This is a true story. Apparently. In 1953, at a Commonwealth Heads of Government luncheon in London, a young Queen Elizabeth was served an Australian marsanne. Imagine, if you will, the scene …

'Pssst. Pssst! I say, Churchill old fellow, what's this they've poured us now? It doesn't taste anything like the usual chablis.'

'Ahem. That, ma'am, is marsanne, ma'am. From Chateau Tahbilk, ma'am. In Orstraylia, ma'am.'

'Oooh, a colonial wine! How exciting! And how nice! I must say I'm rather enjoying it … oh, yes, thank you very much, I will have just a drop more.'

The rest, as they say … Apparently, the Queen was so taken with this glorious golden wine from Down Under that it's been a regular fixture on the House of Commons wine list ever since.

The soft, honeysuckle-flavoured white grape marsanne has been grown in Australia for 200 years. So has its crisper, leaner cousin, roussanne. They both originated in the Rhone Valley in France and were popular with nineteenth-century wineries like Tahbilk in the Goulburn Valley and Yeringberg in the Yarra Valley.

In the last few years, as consumers, writers and marketers have grown thirsty for new tastes and experiences, marsanne and roussanne have enjoyed a resurgence in popularity. They have also been joined by another Rhone variety, viognier, whose dried apricot flavours and exotic, fat, oily texture have really caught the imagination of many winemakers.

In fact, viognier has become a bit of a cult thing in Australia, rather eclipsing marsanne and roussanne. Every time I walk into a winery these days, it seems, I'm handed a glass of pale green liquid and told proudly that it's the winemaker's first attempt with viognier – he planted a hectare or so a couple of years ago, and this is his first crop.

The more examples I taste, the more I'm convinced that viognier – and marsanne and roussanne – are fundamentally warm climate grapes. They seem to need the heat to develop the richness, fatness and exotic streak that I like in them. I also usually prefer viognier that has been made more like a chardonnay (barrel fermentation and ageing) rather than like a riesling (stainless steel fermentation) because the oak complements the variety's big flavours. But I prefer my marsanne unwooded, so that the delicate blossom aromas can shine unhindered.

As for food – well, the options are again endless. Young, aromatic marsanne likes riesling food – light Asian stuff – while fat barrel aged viognier usually makes me think of exotic gewurz food – although the oak factor means you have to be careful with chilli.

whites

As well as the main grape varieties I've outlined on the previous few pages, there are plenty of others that play less important roles in dry white wine-making in Australia. If I was a sporting kind of chap, prone to lazing about in front of the telly on a summer's afternoon, sipping cold beer and watching men dressed in matching outfits try to hit a red leather ball with a bit of wood, then I'd be tempted to lump the following grapes under a pithy title like The Second Eleven. But I'm not that kind of guy, so you'll have to make do with the unglamorous but functional 'Misc.'.

Pinot Gris

By far the trendiest of the Australian Misc. varieties is pinot gris, also known as pinot grigio. Broadly speaking, this grape comes in two guises: early-picked, simple, fruity unwooded white modelled on the pinot grigio of northern and central Italy, and later-picked, fatter, spicier white wine (sometimes barrel aged) which takes its key from the sometimes incredibly rich pinot gris wines of Alsace in France. The pinot gris/grigio thing has only been trendy for about ten years in this country, so it's still early days, but some encouragingly delicious wines have been made in cooler regions like southern Victoria and Tasmania. A couple of people are also playing with more obscure Italian white grapes like arneis and cortese, but again it's early days. Amusingly, the popularity of Italian wine styles has prompted some winemakers proudly to market a dry white made from their trebbiano grapes – which has to be one of the blandest wine grapes in the world.

Verdelho

Hot on the trend heels of pinot gris in the Misc. race (and far more popular in terms of bottles sold) is verdelho. Now, verdelho is a classic case of historical accident come good. It was planted by the nineteenth-century vignerons as a grape for making fortified wines (it originated on the Atlantic island of Madeira), but was soon roped into performing in table wines. Made as a dry white (or, more commonly, a medium-dry white), it can be full of non-specific tropical fruit (a suggestion of pineapple, a whiff of mango), with very appealing, clean, soft gluggability. No one quite knows why, but verdelho has become very popular over the last few years, and is selling out at cellar doors, particularly in the Hunter Valley, McLaren Vale and Western Australia, where it performs best. Personally, I like my verdelho to be as dry as possible, and I like to drink it as young and crisp as I can, although some people reckon it can age as well as semillon.

Chenin Blanc

McLaren Vale and Western Australia, especially the Swan Valley, are also where you'll find a lot of chenin blanc – and you might even find some of it quite drinkable. Chenin, when it's good, is characterised by its high acid and apple-like flavour, but this can, if the vineyard manager and wine-maker aren't careful, turn into a rather flabby and unappealing apple sauce-like flavour. That high acid means that chenin can age very well in the bottle – as anybody who's tried an old Houghton's White Burgundy (now called HWB and originally a chenin-dominant blend) from the Swan Valley will tell you. It's not all age-worthy splendour, though – much of Australia's chenin is planted in the warm inland regions and goes into cheaper blends in bottle or cask, often with colombard – which is also quite widely grown and is usually very boring, although a couple of producers (Primo Estate, Ingoldby spring to mind) manage to make nicely juicy, aromatic wine out of it.

After that, things begin to get a little obscure. There are still resilient plantings of varieties whose importance to the wine industry has come and definitely gone. In western Victoria the rather broad-tasting varieties chasselas and ondenc were once crucial to the early Swiss settlers and sparkling winemakers but are now almost extinct. In Rutherglen, a couple of people persist with the very dull variety gouais (so dull, in fact, that it's been banned in France). And in the Clare Valley the crisp, light crouchen, once widely planted and known as Clare riesling, has fallen from favour.

Because of Australia's huge mid-twentieth-century sherry industry, the established warmer regions still have plantings of the sherry grapes doradillo, palomino and pedro ximinez (or PX). But while the remaining handful of serious sherry-style producers prize these old vineyards – especially the palomino and PX – most of the fruit ends up anonymously blended into casks.

There are tiny pockets of other not terribly good grapes all over the country – dribbles of taminga, for example, a grape developed by Australian scientists in 1970 which, to my taste at least, is quite ghastly – but I'd be here all day if I listed them all.

Before we leave the white grapes alone, though, it's worth mentioning muscat gordo blanco and sultana – gordo and sully – the multi-purpose grapes that can either be sold fresh at the market, dried, or commandeered by a wine industry desperate for fruit, depending on which stage of the economic cycle we're at. There's still plenty of these grapes around.

whites

fizz

Australians have a staggering appetite for sparkling wine. During the gold rush of the 1850s and the boom period of the 1880s, champagne was imported in incredible amounts – the late nineteenth-century streets of Melbourne, according to one disdainful observer, were a morass of mud and broken champagne bottles. Many pioneer vignerons tried to slake this thirst for fizz by coming up with Australian versions, and by the beginning of the twentieth century, local 'champagne' producers were extolling the recuperative virtues of their 'sparkling hock' and 'sparkling burgundy' in the pages of fashionable magazines.

When the wine boom began again in the 1960s the incredibly egalitarian idea of 'champagne' for all was developed. Brands like Great Western, Minchinbury, Seaview and Carrington took the public by storm – 'champagne'-style wines made from any number of grapes like semillon, trebbiano, even decolourised shiraz. These were cheap wines, everyday wines, wines for celebrating Tuesday morning with. If you wanted to crack a bottle of serious bubbly – to celebrate something big, like winning the Melbourne Cup – you went for the French stuff.

That began to change in the early 1980s, when vineyards full of chardonnay and pinot noir began producing serious crops in the trendy new cool climate regions. Winemakers were quick to realise it was no accident that these two grapes are the main ones used in Champagne (the place) to make champagne (the wine): they brought a level of finesse and delicacy to sparkling wine that semillon and decolourised shiraz never could bring. Add Champagne's third grape variety, pinot meunier, and you had all the necessary ingredients for crafting serious fizz that would compete directly with the French.

The new Australian fizz masters were given a huge vote of confidence in the late 1980s and early 90s when a mob of French champagne houses such as Möet et Chandon, Bollinger and Devaux decided to invest here (the if-you-can't-beat-'em-join-'em approach, obviously). This, arguably, brought the technical know-how and tricks of the trade to add to the already highly developed Australian knack for blending (a crucial skill if you're making bubbly). The only way you could improve Australian fizz now was by sourcing better fruit.

Which is precisely what happened. By the end of the 1990s, the big story in Australian sparkling wine was the development of vineyards specifically for fizz production in some of Australia's chilliest places – Macedon, the Adelaide Hills, the Alpine country in Victoria's north-east and especially Tasmania. The quality of our top bubblies improves each year, but the trickle-down effect is also having a positive impact on the cheaper, Tuesday morning bubbly, too. Being able to get good sparkling wine made from chardonnay and pinot noir for around $10 is about as close to the ideal of 'champagne' for all as it's possible to get.

Fizz in the vineyard

This is where Australia's incredibly free wine laws really come into their own. Almost all the best fizz produced in this country – and certainly all the cheapest – is a blend of fruit from different regions, sometimes many different regions, often regions at opposite corners of a state, or even opposite corners of the country. The Australian sparkling winemaker is the ultimate magpie, pilfering batches of chardonnay here, truckloads of pinot there, and slowly building up a nest of flavours.

Having said that, you don't just want grapes from anywhere. You need pinot noir and chardonnay with good flavour but fairly low alcohol (11 per cent or so) and still with fresh, clean acidity. Which is why the long, slow, cool ripening periods you get in Tasmania and the southern Yarra Valley and Tumbarumba are becoming renowned for producing fizz grapes.

Pinot noir, chardonnay and meunier aren't the only varieties used for good fizz. In the Eden Valley, Jim Irvine grows a very obscure grape called meslier and makes a lovely, crisp green apple wine from it. Some winemakers are playing with pinot gris as part of the blend, and others have made varyingly successful fizz from riesling, chenin blanc and sauvignon blanc.

Fizz in the winery

Okay, so you've got your lovely, zesty cool-climate chardonnay and pinot noir. Now what're you going to do? You're going to treat it just like the winemakers in Champagne do, that's what: ferment it cold to make a dry white wine, then stick it in a bottle with a little yeast and sugar, bang on a crown seal, bung it in a cool dark place for eighteen months (or more) for the bubble-forming secondary fermentation to happen and the flavours to develop as the wine spends time in contact with the dead yeast cells, then disgorge it, cork it, wrap the wire and foil on the top and sell it. Simple. Unless you're producing hundreds of thousands of cases of the same wine, in which case you'll probably let the secondary fermentation happen under pressure in a big tank and you won't bother waiting the full eighteen months.

The techniques are pretty much the same wherever you go. What's different is the vineyards the winemaker has chosen the fruit from and the way each parcel of wine is blended with the others.

Fizz in the bottle

Because we don't really have well-defined regional differences in our sparkling wines, the Australian fizz industry has developed clear 'house' styles instead – the full, round, darker-coloured, yeasty characters of Domaine Chandon, Hardys' 'Arras' and Hanging Rock, for example, are a world away from the elegance, finesse and crispness of Petaluma's 'Croser', Piper's Brook's 'Pirie' and the top wines from Seppelt. And it's all to do with the blending.

For a while there, as the premium fizz market developed, almost all the top wines were sold as vintage releases – meaning they were effectively the product of just one year's harvest – to distinguish them from the cheaper, non-vintage wines. Recently, as the market has matured and the prices of the top wines have edged up to French champagne levels, many of the top companies have released a non-vintage wine to sit somewhere between their prestige cuvée and the sea of cheap bubbly.

On the whole, most Australian fizz is close to or at its best when it's released, two years or so after vintage (three or even four years for the very best wines). In only a few cases will it improve dramatically in the bottle – unless it's kept on its lees, and disgorged later, in which case it can improve over ten or more years.

Fizz in the belly

The lighter, crisper, more delicate styles of fizz are the ones that go best with standing around waiting for the speeches to begin, nibbling on little bits of toast with slithers of salty fish on them – or with a big platter of plump Tasmanian oysters drizzled with lime juice and sprinkled with freshly ground black pepper. The fuller, rounder styles are for sitting down to dinner with: smoked salmon, grilled salmon, slow-roasted salmon, that kind of thing. And the cheaper styles are for Tuesday mornings – or Friday afternoons or Saturday lunchtime, or …

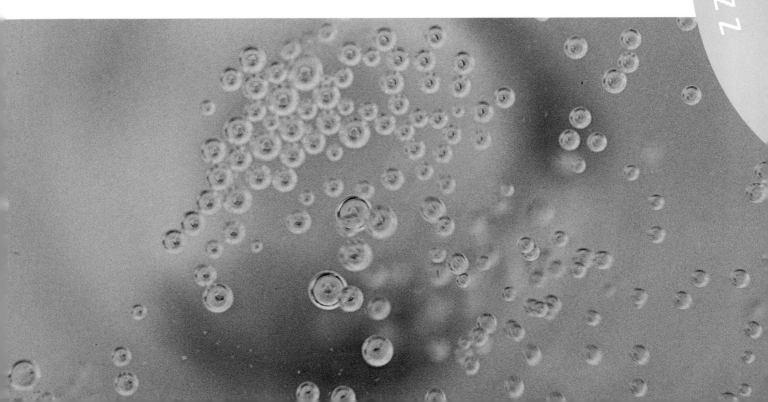

Now I realise that this may be totally impractical, but I want you to see if you can go out and procure yourself a baby emu – preferably a couple of months old and preferably already dead and plucked. There is method in my madness, you'll see. (Get a duck if you can't find an emu.)

Sparkling red may not be absolutely unique to Australia (they produce rather a lot of red fizzy wine in Italy, for example), but the traditional style of sparkling red developed here over a century ago certainly is. Take extremely ripe red grapes – preferably shiraz, but any variety will do as long as it's pregnant with flavour – and put it through the 'champagne' method described above: secondary fermentation in bottle, ageing in cool dark cellars, that kind of thing. When you disgorge it, top it up with some sugary wine to give it a touch of round sweetness. Then, even though it's a red wine, make sure it's served chilled.

To some, this may sound like madness. But Australians love their sparkling red – now. They took to it with gusto in the first half of the twentieth century, but lost interest a bit when the white wine boom took off in the 1970s, and almost lost interest entirely when some bright spark decided to market a really sweet version of sparkling red under the name 'Cold Duck'. In the last decade, though, a new, younger generation have rediscovered it with a passion – which must give the generation of veteran sparkling red drinkers the odd pang of nostalgic pleasure.

Interestingly, winemakers never lost the faith – they just went into the closet when the style fell out of favour, producing enough only for friends and other winemakers, biding their time until the renaissance.

Very 'serious' wine people tend to look down their noses at sparkling red; anything that's *that* much fun couldn't possibly be a great wine. But I love the stuff. Especially with food, and especially with game.

Which brings me back to your baby emu (or duck – all right, it's probably a duck). Bung the lovely thing in the oven and roast it, then serve with large flutes of the best sparkling red you can afford. I think you may end up thanking me. In fact, I know you will.

Stickies

The year 1982 was a momentous one for Australian dessert chefs. It was the year Darren De Bortoli made the first botrytis-affected semillon at his family's large winery at Griffith in New South Wales' Riverina district – a development that changed the whole sweet sticky wine scene overnight.

Australian winemakers had been churning out stickies for years, of course; indeed, Brown Brothers had been making botrytis-affected wines since 1970, and a few were doing really exciting things with botrytis-affected riesling in South Australia in the early 80s. But nobody had ever before made something so clearly modelled on the sweet white wines of Sauternes, in Bordeaux – nor anything so uncannily similar in flavour. Restaurants and wine drinkers went crazy for the new wine, and Australia's dessert chefs were thrown into whirling dervishes of inspiration trying to come up with dishes to match the luscious complexity of the De Bortoli 'sauternes' (as it was called then). Even though a whole army of botrytis-affected wines followed, the De Bortoli 'Noble One' botrytis semillon (as it's called now) is still the commander in chief.

(Out of interest, it's worth recording that the first time I drank the now-legendary 1982 was in 1991, out of the bottle, sitting on a rooftop one night in South London at the end of a particularly eventful party, watching a now-famous wine writer do his Dick Van Dyke routine from *Mary Poppins*. I've been dying to put that in a book somewhere and now I have.)

Botrytis is the so-called 'noble rot', a mould that can, if the conditions are right, produce superbly rich wine from white grapes like semillon by shrivelling them, concentrating the sugar, and adding a layer of apricotty complexity of its own. So many sweet wines on the market are now produced using botrytis that it's easy to forget Australian winemakers did very well without it for years, by merely harvesting its grapes late.

When riesling was the number one grape, it was often made like this, the sugar-rich grapes being turned into 'spatlese' whites (borrowing names from the Old World again – in this case Germany: spatlese means late picking). The Hunter Valley developed its own sweet white wine style called 'porphyry', named after an old Hunter vineyard, and made from late harvest semillon. And today, cheaper late harvest wines are often made from muscat de frontignac – or fronti – an aromatic grape that lends itself to sweeter styles.

Actually a whole host of white grape varieties are called on to produce sweet wines in Australia: orange muscat (really marmaladey flavours), chenin blanc (only occasionally used, which is a shame, as its high acidity can make thrillingly good sticky), chardonnay (not all that often, either, which is not such a bad thing), even the newly trendy grapes pinot gris and viognier.

Some winemakers have also adopted weird and wonderful methods to make sweet wines: Adam Wynn of Mountadam has his truly kooky Ratafia wines, for example (grape juice with spirit added and left to mature in old barrels), and Charlie Melton is experimenting with an Italian-influenced 'vin santo' style – viscous, sherry-like and power- fully sweet.

There's no doubt, though, that the best grapes for stickies are still semillon and riesling – espe- cially if botrytis is involved.

Stickies in the vineyard

Sugar is the key, obviously, to making sweet wines. You need lots of it – which means getting your grapes very ripe indeed. For this reason, a lot of semillon for Australian stickies is grown in warm regions, like the Riverina in New South Wales, where they get the perfect combination of ripeness (lots of sugar), humid mornings (to promote botry- tis growth) and dry afternoons (to stop the botrytis getting out of control). In the Clare Valley, where dry riesling does so well, some grapes are left to hang for longer and pick up botrytis, producing some wonderfully intense wines. Some riesling is left to hang until the first frosts in late May, early June in the country's coldest regions such as Orange and Tasmania, when the grapes freeze on the vine and are occasionally made into 'ice wine'.

Stickies in the winery

Because of its crisp, delicate flavours, sweet riesling is made in a similar fashion to dry riesling: cold fermentation in stainless steel and early bottling. Botrytis semillon, which produces a much more luscious, mouth-coating wine, is often aged in new oak barrels before bottling, giving it an extra layer of complexity. Either way, making sweet white wine can be very hard: the sheer volume of sugar and acid and flavour in the crushed grape juice can give many poor fragile yeast cells the heebie jeebies, and they need to be coaxed into performing.

Stickies in the bottle

If you wanted to criticise Australian sweet wines, especially the semillons, you'd be inclined to say that they are unsubtle: too sweet, too cloying, too much of a good thing. Most of the time I'd tend to agree; on the whole I prefer the juicy zestiness of good botrytis riesling. But then I have a good older semillon from a good producer with the appropriate food, and I have to be mopped up off the floor. Think of them less as fine wines, then, and more as portals into a world of unbridled hedonism – as huge outpourings of affection for the tongue. (Which is one of the reasons why they're mostly bottled in half bottles: any more would just be too dangerous.)

Stickies in the belly

And the appropriate food is? Try to describe the flavours of an Australian sticky and you'll get a few clues. A good sweet semillon, for example, can taste of grilled peaches, and honey, and vanilla ice cream and butter biscuits … there you go, match made. A good sweet riesling, on the other hand, is much more about limes and passionfruit and maybe a touch of lemon curd … see? Now all you need is the pastry and you've got yourself a tart.

Fortifieds

All right, fess up. Who let the cat out of the bag? Who told the Americans how good Australian muscat and tokay can be? Whoever it was, they deserve a spanking, because they've ruined it for the rest of us.

There we are, quietly slurping our way through Rutherglen's finest molasses-like tokays and treacle-like muscats, patting ourselves on the back over what bargains these venerable old liquids are, when Bill Chambers' best wines get near-perfect 99 out of 100 point scores in *Wine Spectator*, one of the most influential wine mags in the world. And what happens? Suddenly the price has rocketed up and you can't get your hands on a bottle for love or money. Still, I suppose it was only a matter of time. We couldn't have kept the secret forever.

As I've told you already in the historical rant at the beginning of this book, fortified wines have played a huge role in Australia's history. For much of the twentieth century, it was cheap and reliable Australian 'port' and 'sherry' they were drinking in bars in Sydney and Sydenham, not cheeky unwooded chardonnay. If practice makes perfect, then, it's no wonder Australian winemakers do such a good job with fortifieds: they've had plenty of experience.

They've also got an invaluable asset in old vineyards full of the right varieties in the right (warm) spots. The only thing they don't have is an enthusiastic and appreciative audience. Sure, there are the rave reviews in American magazines, but, to be serious, they're only for the really pricey stuff; and sure, there are still plenty of people buying their flagons of cheap port in supermarket bottle shops right across the country, but in the middle ground, the popularity of fortified wine isn't exactly booming.

Marketing departments have tried funky bottles, groovy labels, silly names, and occasionally you get a surge of interest, but it never becomes a trend. And a trend is what we want.

I'm trying my best to keep the home fires burning, but there's only so much sherry one man can drink. So come on, be a patriotic Australian. Do your bit for the country by getting out there and buying a bottle of fortified today.

Yet another word about the names. As I think I may have told you already, in 1994 the Australian wine industry came to an arrangement with the European Community that it would stop using European wine names in exchange for freer trade. This means that words like *port*, *sherry* and *tokay* are in the process of being eradicated from Australian wine labels (they haven't been used for export labels for years). Having said that, though, there's nothing stopping *me* using these names for the sake of easy communication, so that's what I've done (partly because the winemakers themselves are yet to come up with any really catchy alternatives I could have used instead).

Muscat and Tokay

These are the twin peaks of fortified wine production in Australia. They are made in many of the country's older warm regions, but find their most orgasmic expression in Rutherglen, in north-east Victoria, where there are barrels of muscat and tokay dating back to the nineteenth century.

The two wines are made in pretty much the same way. Incredibly ripe, almost raisined grapes are picked as late as possible and crushed (or rather sludged). Fermentation is begun, but before much of the sugar has been converted into alcohol, spirit is added to stop fermentation. Then the resulting strong, sweet wine is put into old barrels to mature for years, sometimes decades, turning brown in colour and picking up richness, depth and complexity as it ages.

The main differences between the two styles, then, lie in the grape varieties used. Muscat is made from the dark-coloured brown muscat grape and produces slightly reddish wines of ultra-sweet, marmaladey, raisiny, spicy, coffee character; whereas tokay is made from muscadelle, a white grape which produces more yellow/tawny wines with flavours of toffee, malt and dark honey. I like both, depending on which side of midnight I'm drinking them, and whether there's sticky date pudding or orange cake on the plate in front of me.

The muscat producers of Rutherglen have recently decided on a

fortifieds

four-tier system of quality classification for their wines, to give the consumer an idea of what's in the bottle before they buy. At the bottom of the pyramid is straight Rutherglen Muscat – up-front, youthful, easy drinking wines; then there's Classic Muscat – wines with a little more complexity and depth; then we have Grand Muscat – great complexity, much more aged, rancio characters; and finally, tiny quantities of Rare Muscat – unbeatable, extraordinary, hedonistic, powerful, died-and-gone-to-heaven lusciousness.

At the tasting to launch the classification the producers opened a bottle of every muscat produced in the region. By the time I'd worked my way round the room, I was licking my sticky fingers and gibbering with joy. You taste the top wines, the incredibly deep and complex Rare Muscats, and you just can't help feeling that you're tasting perfection. I mean really: how could it get any better than this?

Sherry

Talk about polarised. At one end of the sherry market in Australia you have large quantities of cheap, reliable but essentially uninteresting wine that sells well, and at the other, you have a handful of (and I really do mean four or five) passionate, dedicated producers like James Godfrey at Seppelt and Chris Pfeiffer at Pfeiffer still crafting small batches of excellent sherry that doesn't exactly walk out of the door.

All the major styles of sherry are produced in Australia, from quite dry to very sweet, but my favourites are the pale, dry, fino style, influenced by the salty, tangy flor yeast that forms in the barrels, and the light amber-coloured, grilled-hazelnut-tasting amontillado style with its lingering savoury flavours (both are slightly more fruity and sweeter than their Spanish counterparts).

I can't recommend these wines highly enough. They are great with tapas-style tucker: olives, salty fish, peppers, meatballs, oysters. They also go surprisingly well with Japanese food. Hmmm. I'm fighting an uphill battle here, aren't I? I'm never going to get you to try Australian sherry, am I?

No worries. All the more for me.

Port

Once upon a time, this country floated on a sea of port. In the middle of the twentieth century it was virtually all we drank. In the 1970s and 80s we went crazy for series of collectors vintage ports, wines that were guaranteed to build in value with age (they haven't). Today, we might not be drinking quite as much of it, but port still plays a fairly important role in the industry.

There are two broad styles of Australian port: tawny and vintage (affectionately known as VP). The tawny style is usually made predominantly from grenache and shiraz, is aged in barrel for many years, to develop its distinctive tawny colour and spicy, woody flavour, and is usually a blend of many different vintages. The best Australian tawnies, fifty or a hundred years old, can be hauntingly beautiful wines: sometimes deceptively pale tan in colour, sometimes as dark as tar, but always packing an incredible punch of intense, nutty, smoky complexity that forces you to face up to your own mortality (as in: this wine will still taste fantastic when I'm pushing up the daisies).

The VP style, on the other hand, is the product of a single year, and is bottled after spending only a year or so in barrel, before it has lost its deep purple colour. Traditionally, the major grape used for Australian VP was shiraz and the wines produced were hugely unsubtle, dark, sweet, in-your-face blockbusters. But in recent years, most serious VP makers have moved towards Portuguese port varieties like touriga and are making more refined wines – still big and powerful, but a tad more subtle and drier on the finish. Each vintage sees big improvements, and this is an area worth watching.

Just don't tell the Americans.

Australia's
WineRegions
&Winemakers

A Sense of Place

Australia is a staggeringly huge country. I know you know that, but it really is an important thing to fix in your mind when you're thinking about Australian wine. You need to get your head around the fact that a powerful, rich shiraz from a shimmering hot inland vineyard along the Murray River, and a wispy, perfumed riesling from a cold gravelly vineyard in southern Tasmania, and an intense, oatmeal-and-melon flavoured chardonnay from a breezy, gum-tree-fringed vineyard in Margaret River are all products of the same industry.

I find this idea mind-boggling, sometimes. As I raced around working on this book, the country's vastness would occasionally crowd in at the car window and send me off into a gentle panic attack. We'd be hurtling along yet another dead-straight road in far south-west Western Australia, four hours away from the next vineyard, and I'd make the mistake of looking at the map. I felt like we were in a Cinemascope wilderness, yet according to the map we were barely scratching along the edge.

Vintage starts each year in January, in the very hot regions of Roma in Queensland, in the Swan Valley in Western Australia, and at lonely Chateau Hornsby near Alice Springs, the Northern Territory's only winery. For the next five months, as the harvest rumbles slowly across the land, somebody somewhere in Australia is picking grapes and turning them into wine.

As the grapes grow in each region, a number of factors peculiar to that point on the globe – climate and soil, how many grapes are hanging on the vine, how the vine is managed, and so on – will contribute to the flavour and quality of the resulting wine. Different conditions in another region – even in a vineyard just up the road in the same region – will produce different flavours and quality.

In other words, fermented grape juice from one place can convey a unique sense of that place to the drinker. (Another mind-boggling concept, I know.)

This idea (let's pigeonhole it and call it regionalism) is pretty exciting stuff. It's certainly been a hot topic for winemakers for the last decade or so. It was brought into sharp focus by a 1994 trade agreement between Australia and the European Community, whereby Australia had to register its wine zones and regions as Geographical

Indications, or GIs (zones are big GIs that sit above regional GIs – the Port Phillip zone around Melbourne, for example, contains the regions of Yarra Valley, Mornington Peninsula, Geelong, Macedon and Sunbury).

So now, if I sell a bottle of wine in London with Barossa Valley written on the label, I would be breaking the law if that wine didn't come from within the clearly defined boundaries of the Barossa Valley. More importantly, some people argue, if I sell a wine with Barossa Valley on the label, I should be trying to make sure it tastes like it comes from the Barossa Valley.

This defining of the regions has caused the odd kerfuffle among winemakers ('Go on, let me be in your gang.' 'No, you're on the wrong side of the road – and anyway, you said nasty things about my brother.' 'Did not.' 'Did too…') but it has mostly been a smooth (if slow) process. Focussing on what makes one region's wines special has also helped the development of wine tourism in many rural areas of Australia and increased awareness of the diversity of Australian wine styles.

Having said all that, though, you have to keep reminding your-self that most of the wine in the drive-through grog shop attached to my local pub is a blend of grapes from many different wine-growing districts. 'South-Eastern Australia' is the GI you'll most often find on labels – which means that the grapes could have come from almost anywhere in the country.

In a climate of fervent regionalism, such promiscuity can be frowned upon. But the freedom to blend between regions and grape varieties actually creates a remarkably consistent product at the bottom end, and has resulted in some classic wines over the decades – the combination of Barossa shiraz and Coonawarra cabernet, both great in their own right, is legendary. In fact, the freedom to blend should be enshrined in the Australian winemaker's bill of rights – not that there is one, mind you, but if there was it should be.

Big Vineyards

Big Rivers

1 Sunraysia
2 Riverland
3 Swan Hill
4 Riverina

2

1

Griffith •

4

Mildura •

3

If you want to give somebody a good
feel for the massive business end of
the Australian wine industry, you
fly them straight into Mildura in the
hot north-west of Victoria in late

summer. As the plane descends, the endless brown, sunbaked land gives
way to vast patches of green – vineyards stretching away into the distance
as far as you can see. The field of green is broken only by the mighty River
Murray, snaking its way through the vines, and by occasional, enormous,
gleaming wineries.

You get in a car, whack up the air-con and drive. For hours you're
whizzing past vine row after vine row, thick trunks and lush green
canopy laden with grapes bursting out of the pinky-red sandy soil. Then,
suddenly, as soon as you leave the irrigated areas, you're heading
through scrubby dry outback again, with country music and talkback
crackling through on the car radio.

To get a feel for how much wine is produced here, you visit Lindemans
Karadoc winery, one of Australia's largest, and you gawk at the endless
stream of trucks coming in, laden with fruit. This place is a magnet for
grapes. They crush 100 tonnes an hour here during the height of vintage
– over 2000 tonnes a day. That's more than some of Australia's smaller
regions produce each *year*.

The scale of it freaks me out every time I come here – it'd scare the living bejesus out of your average small winemaker used to grappling with a
hectare of vines in Tasmania. But this is undeniably the heart of Australian
wine.

Here, in the Sunraysia district around Mildura; further down the Murray
into Victoria, towards Echuca; across the border in South Australia's
Riverland, around Renmark and Kingston; and over in the Riverina, near
Griffith in New South Wales – between them, these Big River irrigated
regions produce three quarters of Australia's annual crush. Millions of cases
of wine are trucked out of here each year. Which is why I've put them up the
front: they're important. And they are improving all the time.

Australians are obsessed with water. Not surprising, really, since they
are surrounded by the stuff. Yet while they live and play on it, they see
very little of it fall from the sky. So when somebody came up with a scheme

to turn desert sand into farmland, people must have thought he was mad – but they jumped at the chance to give it a go.

The land around the River Murray had all the right attributes for growing great fruit – almost limitless sunshine, fertile soils, cool nights. But it lacked that one essential ingredient: constant water. The river would either flood or nearly dry up completely, depending on the time of year.

George and William Chaffey had seen irrigation bring life to similarly thirsty lands in California, and when they arrived in Australia in 1887 they set about trying to achieve the same results along the Murray. The scheme didn't become fully operational, though, until locks were installed along the River in 1920, bringing about real control of the water.

By the time the export boom for fortified wines to England took off in the 1930s, the vineyard regions of both the Murray and Murrumbidgee rivers were well placed to supply. Equally, when the cask wine market exploded in the 1970s, the big vineyards were able to adapt, turning their sultana grapes into cheap and cheerful white plonk for the silver bladders. This is when the big, technologically advanced table wine-focussed wineries like Lindemans Karadoc were built – just in time to start working up to the export boom of the late 80s.

In the 1990s, a more fundamental shift took place in the irrigated areas. For a start, many of the low-quality, multi-purpose grapes like sultana (sully to its friends) were steadily replaced with 'premium' varieties – predominantly chardonnay and shiraz. Quality-conscious producers like Deakin Estate, Kingston Estate and Trentham Estate realised that by cutting back on the irrigation a little, the vines would produce fewer, smaller bunches of grapes – of a higher quality.

So even though this is still a huge bulk- and cask-wine producing area, the last couple of years have seen unprecedented developments – like four-litre casks of chardonnay (a grape that didn't even figure on the official planting statistics just a quarter of a century ago), and Riverland shiraz and merlot produced from low-yielding vines for sale at over $30 a bottle.

(There is an added incentive to reduce water use up here, of course. The Murray–Darling river system is under constant pressure, and soil salinity is a very real problem in the area. Making sure that viticulture is sustainable in this climate makes not only good environmental sense but good business sense, too.)

Kingston Estate's Bill Moularadellis is particularly keen to explore and take pride in the region's potential by planting and making new grape varieties. He's trialing the ultra-hip white grape, viognier, and is very keen on the late-ripening, dark-coloured red grape, petit verdot, both of which are normally associated with much trendier cool regions down south or out west. His enthusiasm is rubbing off, too: others are branching out into all sorts of new styles.

Some are going the other way, though, by rediscovering the district's heritage. As Stefano di Pieri, chef at the Grand Hotel in Mildura, pointed out to the world in his hit TV show, *A Gondola on the Murray*, there are patches of fifty-year-old grenache and mourvedre up here, and old olive groves, and traditional Italian food producers ... a regional identity, in other words, every bit as strong as the Barossa or Margaret River.

Big River flavours

The most familiar Australian wine flavour in the world, the one that hundreds of thousands of drinkers across the globe experience every day, is chardonnay from the Big Rivers. Ripe, easy, sun-filled fruit flavour, spiced up with a lick of vanilla oak (picked up from the somewhat unglamorous bags of oak chips I mentioned earlier). This is a world away from the

finesse of chardonnay from the Adelaide Hills or the richness of chardonnay from the Hunter, but it's incredibly – and deservedly – popular. Not complex, not deep, not long-tasting – but friendly.

There is plenty of verdelho, semillon, colombard and chenin blanc up here, too (even, as I've said, the odd patch of viognier), producing plenty of clean, crisp, simple fruity white wine, but sultana and muscat gordo blanco still occupy much of the vineyard area – although their importance is declining.

Traditionally, River reds have been pretty limp things: good colour but faint varietal flavour, low impact in the mouth, and short. In the last few years, now that more effort is being made and better varieties are being used, quality has really improved – not everywhere, but certainly in enough pockets to make it a trend.

Shiraz is the most popular choice, with some really dark, ripe, soft wines emerging, followed closely by cabernet sauvignon and merlot, which can be surprisingly good. There is still a fair amount of grenache and mourvedre here, giving spice and life to blends, as well as the dark-coloured chambourcin and ruby cabernet giving – well, colour. As I've said, there are also winemakers with faith in petit verdot, sangiovese and even tempranillo. The Rivers are definitely worth watching.

Everything Old is New Again

New South Wales

New South Wales Wine Regions

1 Riverina
2 Tumbarumba
3 Canberra
4 Hilltops
5 Cowra
6 Orange
7 Mudgee
8 Hunter Valley

Sydney •

• Canberra

Who decided that the vast, sun-drenched bush-covered mountain country around Sydney looked like Wales? They must have been on drugs. Have you ever been to Wales? There are mountains, sure, and the odd bit of wide open space, and lots of sheep, but gum trees? Bushfires? Sub-tropical heat? I think not. It's out and out Australian.

New South Wales is often referred to as Australia's first wine-producing state, the cradle of viticulture. I prefer to think of it as Australia's *biggest* wine producing state – not in terms of production (although it pumps out a lot of booze), but in terms of distance. As well as the centrally located historic regions like the Hunter Valley and Mudgee, there are vineyards scattered all over the state: right up in the north, near the Queensland border, right down in the south, near the Victorian border, and right over in the western corner, spilling over the border into South Australia. There are even vines (the first to be picked in the world each year) in the parched middle of the state, literally out back o' Bourke.

Most of these vineyards are relatively new, too. Cassegrain winery's success with the humidity-tolerant red variety chambourcin has attracted a small flock of winemakers to the coast along the Hastings River north of Sydney and the Shoalhaven River south of the state capital. There is a buzz in the industry, too, about the grapes being grown right up north near Tenterfield. Some vineyards are even dotted around Sydney again, where most of the early grape growers gave up the fight with the heat, humidity and phylloxera over a century ago.

Dan Dineen,
winemaker,
Tower Estate

Iain Riggs (top) and
PJ Charteris (bottom),
winemakers,
Brokenwood Wines

acknowledged that the Hunter is the godfather of regionalism in this country, and are paying their respects. The old, traditional companies like Tyrrell's and McWilliam's are finally being given credit for keeping their strongest assets – namely some wonderful old vineyards and wine styles that are unique in the world of wine. And that other big old company, Lindemans, has been given a totally new lease of life by its owners, Southcorp, with wine quality improving dramatically over the last couple of years.

A growing band of small producers are also trying to establish a new tradition. In many cases, these new producers are winemakers who have left large companies and set out on their own: David Lowe (ex-Rothbury winemaker), making some lovely wines under the Lowe Family label; Neil McGuigan (ex-Wyndham Estate and McGuigan Brothers), making brilliantly traditional wine at Briar Ridge; and Andrew Margan (ex-Tyrrell's), causing a stir with his Margan Family range of thoroughly Hunter-style wines.

There are brand new names to look out for, too: small, low-profile, high-quality producers like Glenguin, in the Broke-Fordwich sub-region to the east of the Hunter; and more glamorous, high-profile developments like Tower Estate right on the tourist strip in the heart of the valley, combining the entrepreneurial talents of Len Evans and Brian McGuigan, and the skills of up-and-coming winemaker Dan Dineen.

As I say: boom, boom, boom.

Hunter Valley flavours

Despite everything I've said about semillon being this incredibly distinctive, magnificently regional wine, there is actually more chardonnay planted in the Hunter Valley. Hardly surprising, this: Tyrrell's Vat 47 Hunter chardonnay is considered the first commercial example of the variety in the country, and it inspired a wave of planting. The wines can be good, too, in a typically warm-climate style: the best producers, such as Tyrrell's, Scarborough, Mount Pleasant and Allandale, all turn out some of the country's richest chardonnays, full of pineapple fruit and creamy textures.

Verdelho is the third major white variety, and it has enjoyed a burst of popularity of late, with wines from producers such as Tulloch and

Rothbury showing the grape's tropical fruit and off-dry sweetness in all its refreshing juiciness.

It's semillon, though, that purists like me will always reach for in the Hunter. When it's young, unwooded Hunter semillon is lean, crisp and almost neutral in style. But with five, ten years in the bottle, it grows into a glowing yellow, rich-smelling, buttered toast and lemon-flavoured wine with extraordinary personality. Best producers include Tyrrell's (especially Vat 1), Mount Pleasant (Elizabeth and Lovedale), Brokenwood and Briar Ridge, with Lindemans and Rothbury improving in recent years.

Many of the Hunter's wineries make wine using fruit from other regions – mostly stated on the label, but occasionally not. This is because while cabernet and merlot can do well here, they can do much better elsewhere. Pepper Tree, for example, make an excellent merlot from Coonawarra grapes; Brokenwood make a couple of superb McLaren Vale shirazes; and Rothbury have a range of good value wines from Mudgee. Which is all lovely, but it's the 100 per cent Hunter shirazes that interest me more – classic, medium-bodied, brick-red wines from the region's naturally low-yielding vineyards.

> It's semillon, though, that purists like me will always reach for in the Hunter. When it's young, unwooded Hunter semillon is lean, crisp and almost neutral in style.

I've struggled for years to find an adequate description for Hunter shiraz. When it's young, it reflects how it's made – if it was matured in big old vats it tends to show more the earthy, plummy flavours; if it was matured in small new barrels then the flavours will be darker, more berryish and, of course, oakier. But there's a character that appears in varying degrees in older Hunter shiraz, regardless of how it was made – a kind of dusty forest floor, old spice cabinets, camphor and clove flavour (and I'm still not convinced that does it justice). Look for Tyrrell's (Vat 9), Brokenwood (Graveyard Vineyard), Mount Pleasant (Rosehill, OP and OH), Rothbury (Brokenback Vineyard) – and if you ever come across old, dusty bottles of Tulloch and Lindemans from the 1960s, buy them and relish their deeply mushroomy flavours.

Upper Hunter

Strictly speaking, the last section should have been called the Lower Hunter Valley, to differentiate it from the Upper Hunter Valley, based around Denman, sixty kilometres or so north-west of Pokolbin. The Upper Hunter is different winegrowing country – warmer, slightly drier, suited far more to whites than reds – and totally different in feel. Where the Lower Hunter is bustling with concentrated vineyard activity and frenetic cellar doors, the Upper Hunter is spread out, full of huge, ranch-like farms and the odd open-cut mine, and is moving at a more sedate pace. Big vineyards have been planted here recently, but it is home to only a handful of wineries.

Recently arrived wineries such as Reynolds Yarraman and Barrington Estate have lifted the profile of the region a little, but it is still very much dominated by the huge Rosemount Estate, whose vineyards and winery at Denman seem to get bigger every time I go there. Indeed, if it weren't for the huge commercial success of Rosemount (and, to a lesser extent the region's other big winery, Arrowfield), especially in export markets, I doubt whether the Upper Hunter would have developed in the way that it has.

The region had vineyards in the nineteenth century but they didn't last. It was re-pioneered in the 1960s by Penfolds, but again, that didn't last. So it was left to Rosemount and its energetic founding family, the Oatleys, to prove what could be done here.

Rosemount now source fruit from and make wines right across the country – McLaren Vale shiraz, Coonawarra cabernet, Orange shiraz, Mudgee cabernet – but their spiritual home is still the Upper Hunter, and their prized chardonnay vineyards at Roxburgh and Giant's Creek. Winemaker Philip Shaw does great things with all his wines, but when you walk through the winery tasting through the barrels, you can't help sensing he feels just a little bit more attached to the barrels of Roxburgh chardonnay.

Upper Hunter flavours

Chardonnay, chardonnay and, um, more chardonnay. That's really what the Upper Hunter is all about. Semillon is planted here, and can occasionally be good, making, in the hands of talented winemakers like Philip

Shaw at Rosemount and Jon Reynolds at Reynolds Yarraman, soft, lemony, toasty white wine that ages surprisingly well. But Upper Hunter chardonnay, particularly from the best Rosemount vineyards, can be very good indeed. Roxburgh is the classic example: golden, buttery, rich wine, with opulent tropical fruit and lots of toasty oak. Giant's Creek is a slightly more restrained, tangy, complex and juicier version of the same song.

A few people persist with red wines although the best reds in the region are made using fruit from outside its boundaries.

Philip Shaw,
winemaker,
Rosemount Estate

My first exposure to Mudgee was in England, just when I was beginning to get into wine. It was an experience that stayed with me for a long time.

Mudgee

Somehow, I'd stumbled across a bottle of old Botobolar Mudgee shiraz. I had read somewhere that this vineyard was run organically, and that wines from the region were traditionally known as Mudgee Mud. When I opened the bottle, I wasn't disappointed: the wine was black, rich, dense and incredibly earthy, like liquid clay. I loved it. It was nothing like the cleaner, fruitier Australian wines I was used to.

I've drunk a lot of Mudgee wine since then, and most of it has been decidedly less muddy. But still, in the best wines – like the reds from Huntington Estate and the monumentally good 'Mountain Blue' shiraz cabernet from Rosemount – I still get flashbacks to the plush, clay-like density of that first experience.

I've visited Mudgee a few times since then, too, and have fallen in love with the place. I once spent a hot summer's Wednesday having a full-on roast Sunday lunch in a faithfully restored Victorian hotel dining room in Mudgee, drinking red wine, and listening to the mayor of the town, a ruddy-faced farmer called Percy, singing bush ballads and reciting Banjo Paterson at length (if only I had a documentary film crew with me, I thought at the time).

There's something about the place that just feels right: the fact that it is so well defined, so clearly contained by a ring of low mountains, a fertile bowl up in the dry country of central New South Wales. No wonder the Aborigines gave the place a name meaning 'nest in the hills'.

Like the Hunter, Mudgee had its nineteenth-century wine pioneers and its gold-rush-related prosperity, but unlike the Hunter, it didn't survive intact into the twentieth century (only one of the original wineries, Craigmoor, carried on making wine in the district – and even that is now owned by Orlando Wyndham and has merged with its larger sister winery, Montrose). Like the Hunter, Mudgee was revived in the late 1960s by a man with a vision – in this case Bob Roberts at Huntington Estate. But unlike the Hunter, Roberts wasn't followed by many imitators – there were others, such as David Robertson at Thistle Hill and Gil Wahlquist at Botobolar, but they amounted to nowhere near the stampede that rushed the Hunter.

Mudgee's more remote, less tourist-oriented position must have played a part in this, because Hunter winemakers have always acknowledged that Mudgee is a better place to grow grapes. Many of them have been trucking Mudgee grapes over the mountains to blend with Hunter wines for years – if not always acknowledging this on their labels.

For most of the 1980s, then, Mudgee plodded along, producing some pretty good wines, but not attracting huge attention. The wine boom of the 1990s, though, has seen Mudgee really begin to pick up the pace. Upper Hunter winery Rosemount Estate moved into the region by establishing vineyards in the early part of the decade, and has since released some very impressive new wines. There are other new developments such as the gleaming Andrew Harris winery south of Mudgee township and some huge vineyard plantings off the main routes. And there are some rediscoveries, such as the Italian varieties sangiovese and barbera, which have been grown at Montrose since the 1970s.

Suddenly, Mudgee is a very exciting place to be.

Mudgee flavours

If shiraz is the wine that has made the Hunter's reputation, then cabernet–shiraz blends are what Mudgee seems particularly good at. Rosemount's 'Mountain Blue' has caused a kerfuffle with its incredibly rich, deep black fruit flavours, but Huntington Estate has been doing exceptionally well with the blend for years. Cabernet on its own can be very good – gutsier and more concentrated than the wines from the Hunter – and shiraz can also do well but I still reckon the best wines are the blends. Mudgee also does well with less mainstream red varieties, producing wines with ripe, round red fruit-gum flavours out of the Italian varieties (Montrose) and encouragingly plush flavours out of merlot (Andrew Harris).

Chardonnay was 'discovered' at Mudgee about the same time Tyrrell's were producing their first wine in the 1970s, and it has made predictably ripe, honeyed, rich white wines ever since, not all that different from Hunter chardonnay. Semillon is also not a million miles away from the Hunter in style: the wines are a little less austere when they're young, with fuller lemon and hay flavours, but on the whole don't age as magnificently.

How chilly does a wine region have to be before it can look you in the eye and unhesitatingly call itself cool climate? Take the Canberra District in southern New South

Canberra

Wales: on paper, looking at the statistics, it's definitely cool – similar, in fact, to the Yarra Valley and Coonawarra, both much further south. It's certainly high up: the vineyards lie between 500 and almost 900 metres above sea level. And during the long autumn the nights can get bitter here, meaning grapes are still being picked into May.

But go there in summer, when the hot sun beats down on the blond, parched paddocks and tin-roof wineries and there hasn't been a drop of rain for weeks, and the vines are gratefully sucking up every drip of irrigation to stay alive. Then taste the wines – rich, full chardonnay at Doonkuna, ripe merlot at Lake George, concentrated cabernet at Kyeema, even powerfully flavoured muscat at Clonakilla – and tell me this place is unhesitatingly cool climate. I know the road signs say it is, but often your palate will disagree.

The point is that it's hard to generalise about the Canberra district. For every one of those ripe tasting wines I just mentioned, for example, there are at least two or three that do fit into the cool climate mould: the crisp rieslings and sparkling wine up at Lark Hill, one of the region's highest vineyards, or Clonakilla's uncompromisingly intense, cool climate version of shiraz.

The region was established tentatively in the early 1970s when Doctor Edgar Riek planted his Lake George vineyard (a stone's throw from Lake George, funnily enough) and Doctor John Kirk planted Clonakilla near Murrumbateman, both about fifteen kilometres north of Canberra. Over the next few years another dozen or so wineries appeared, most, like the first two, a passionate weekend pursuit for Canberra professionals – doctors, academics, former Governors-General. Some of those weekend winemakers, such as David and Sue Carpenter at Lark Hill and Tim Kirk, Doctor John's son, have gone full-time, but for years the region has mostly plodded gently along in first gear.

In 1997, though, all this changed when BRL Hardy announced they were going to invest in Canberra big time, plant 250 hectares of grapes and build a winery. Even the most idealistic and pure small winemakers, normally suspicious of the large companies, had to admit this was a glowing endorsement of Canberra's potential. And in 1999 Clonakilla's shiraz was named best wine at the New South Wales wine awards in Sydney, beating off some incredibly stiff opposition from the state's shiraz heartlands, the Hunter Valley and Mudgee.

So is it a real cool climate or not? Oh, look, who cares? It makes good wine and that's all that matters, surely.

Canberra flavours

Ah, well, now it all depends here on where you are and what the weather's like. There are (at least) three broad sub-regions: the warmest bits around Hall, just north of Canberra; the cooler bits up around Murrumbateman and Yass, to the north of Hall; and the much cooler bits again, over near Lake George and Queanbeyan (and no, I can't pronounce it either). Also, a big warm year can produce flavours quite different to those from a mean, cold year, wherever you are.

Riesling does very well here, especially in the cooler sites, producing floral perfumed wines with great lean acidity – not unlike those from Eden Valley in South Australia. Chardonnay can do well, with crisp citrussy fruit often backed up by lots of nutty, leesy, barrel fermentation complexity (Doonkuna and Lark Hill do well). And the aromatic varieties like sauvignon blanc (often blended with semillon) and viognier (from Clonakilla only) can be in a quite reserved, tight, minerally style.

Pinot noir has done well here, and could be a variety to watch out for in the future, especially in the cooler parts such as Lark Hill's high vine-yard. Far more popular, though, are cabernet sauvignon and merlot, often blended together. In warmer sites like Hall and from warmer vintages, these varieties can produce good, ripe, dark-berried wines; in the cooler parts and cooler vintages they can be a bit mean, minty and green. At the moment, Clonakilla is virtually alone as the region's shiraz producer, but the stunning wine it makes from the variety – blended with a little of the aromatic viognier, and intense, fragrant and full of white pepper, dark cherries and understatement – should encourage more to plant it.

So is it a real cool climate or not?
Oh, look, who cares? It makes good
wine and that's all that matters, surely.

Tim Kirk,
winemaker,
Clonakilla

One of the first articles I wrote as an eager young wine hack in the early 1990s was about Orange. I was at the Hunter Valley wine show awards dinner when the trophy for best cabernet was announced: a wine from Bloodwood in Orange. You could hear the whispers crackle through the audience: 'Who? Where?' The next day, at the exhibitors' tasting, there was a crowd huddled around the cabernet table, with people keen to taste this upstart wine.

Orange then was still a fairly well-kept secret in the wine industry, with only a few aware of the region's exciting potential. A couple of wines like Bloodwood's cabernet had trickled out, and a couple of winemakers in the Hunter Valley had driven in, looking for fruit to buy, but it was still unknown enough to cause a stir at the wine show. Orange now is arguably New South Wales' most exciting region, with only a dozen or so wineries but plenty of vineyard development, and, more importantly, a string of steadily improving wines under its belt.

When Stephen and Rhonda Doyle established the Bloodwood vineyard at Orange in the early 1980s, they were pioneers. It wasn't long, though, before others twigged to the potential of this high-up (800 metres above sea level) central NSW highland region. Its bright, clean air, sloping hillsides and, most importantly, strong continental climate (hot days, cool nights, long autumn) make it a very attractive place for grape growers.

And the grape growers have come – with bells on. Two of the biggest vineyards in the district are those east of the town belonging to the Upper Hunter winery Rosemount, and a huge development of 480 hectares (that's 1200 acres in the old money) at Molong, further north, growing grapes for Southcorp. These companies are far too sensible to go horsing around with a region they didn't have a whole heap of faith in. Aren't they?

The wines that Rosemount have so far released under their Orange vineyard label have been excellent ambassadors for the region. So have those made by Jon Reynolds at another Upper Hunter winery, Reynolds Yarraman. Importantly, these have been relatively widely available. The best of the Orange-based wineries, in comparison – Bloodwood, Canobolas-Smith, Highland Heritage and the recently arrived Brangayne of Orange – each produce only a couple of thousand cases a year, so finding their wines

Hilltops

Things get a little more interesting in the Hilltops region, mostly concentrated around the town of Young. Traditionally, this was stone fruit country, with Young cherries (apparently) enjoying a worldwide reputation, but in the last two decades or so, it has increasingly been invaded by vineyards.

We're higher up here, and the wine styles reflect the shift to a cooler climate. Chardonnay is more intense and finer, and has good, lingering, citrussy elegance. The reds are markedly more successful, too, with good, medium-to-full bodied dark-berryish cabernet, and shiraz that manages to combine the ripeness and fullness of warmer climates with the lifted perfumed spiciness of the cooler spots. There is some zinfandel planted here, too, and I reckon it could do very well in the future, as could the northern Italian varieties.

Like at Orange, there are a couple of small wineries here, but most of the grapes are trucked out to be made by the large companies. The wines from McWilliam's Barwang vineyard, and those produced by Hunter Valley-based wineries Allandale and Hungerford Hill (Southcorp) have done a lot to get the Hilltops message out.

Tumbarumba

We've finally shifted to cool country up here. This spectacular region is fringed by often snow-capped mountains, and the evenings can really bite into your bones as the growing season moves into autumn.

I first visited this place with a sparkling winemaker from one of the large companies. What impressed him – and still impresses many – about Tumbarumba is the region's ability to produce excellent chardonnay and pinot noir for fizz: the cool nights help retain the all-important citrussy lemon acidity. His company and many others take a lot of fruit from here for use – mostly unacknowledged – in their best bubblies.

Since then, though, a few white wines have been released – mostly by Hungerford Hill – that have also really impressed me. Sauvignon blanc is definitely suited to the region, making tangy, pungent, herbaceous, intense wines. Chardonnay can also be great – but reds, apart from pinot noir, struggle to ripen well.

Running in the Family

South Australia

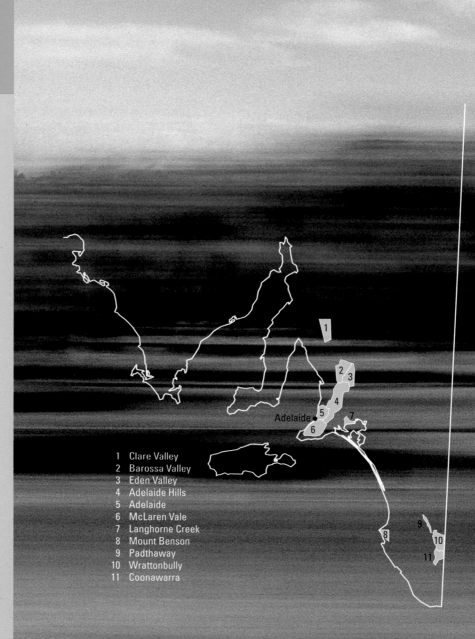

Adelaide

1 Clare Valley
2 Barossa Valley
3 Eden Valley
4 Adelaide Hills
5 Adelaide
6 McLaren Vale
7 Langhorne Creek
8 Mount Benson
9 Padthaway
10 Wrattonbully
11 Coonawarra

South Australians are so proud of their wine industry that they positively glow. With good reason, too: SA is the biggest wine-producing state in the country in terms of output; three out of four of the industry's largest companies are based there; and regions like the Barossa Valley and McLaren Vale have been making wine continuously for over 150 years.

Whenever I go to SA, I feel like everybody I meet knows somebody who works for a winery, or has a relative who's a vineyard manager, or has a vineyard of their own. And those who don't either work in restaurants and drink lots of wine, or their dad's been buying wine from so-and-so in the Clare Valley for donkey's years, or they went to school with the daughter of the bloke that owns the winery. Wine is in their blood.

Even if you only pass through Adelaide, you can't help noticing that there are century-old olive groves in the city's parkland, and that there are thriving wine regions less than an hour's drive away in all directions (except, of course, west, which is inconveniently wet and salty). This is why I love visiting the place: even as an outsider I feel proud of its rich wine culture.

Some South Australians take that pride a little too far, of course, and develop hints of hot-blooded parochialism. (A sure-fire way of getting your head kicked in, for example, would be to stand up on the bar in the Exeter Hotel on Rundle Street on a Saturday night and shout 'Barossa shiraz is for poofters! Real men drink shiraz from the Hunter Valley!') Luckily, most keep their pride down at a warm glow.

Barossa Valley

It's eight o'clock in the morning and I'm standing in the middle of a crowded square, watching a red-faced bloke in traditional Silesian dress trying to auction off a squealing pig. I've got a glass of foaming fermenting shiraz juice in one hand, and a soft bread roll barely containing a plump bratwurst sausage smothered in sauerkraut in the other hand. It doesn't, I think to myself, get much more quintessentially Barossa than this.

You can get addicted to the Barossa Valley, especially if your first exposure to it is during the notorious Barossa Vintage Festival. The Festival, now into its sixth decade, is an enormous event that involves the whole community – all of whom can be seen lining the road for the great procession from Nuriootpa to Tanunda, the Barossa's main towns, each dressed in even more authentically Silesian dress than their neighbour. It's an outrageous festival, full of oompah bands and barrel-rolling and jazz in the vineyards and grand dinners. It's fun, but boy, is it tiring – so tiring, in fact, that the Barossans can only bring themselves to hold it every other year.

You don't have to go to the Barossa at festival time to see that wine is woven into the fabric of the place – and that it's woven in a thoroughly Teutonic design. The influence of the Silesian settlers who came here in the 1840s can't be underestimated. It can't be easily avoided, either: you see it on the road signs, on the winery signs, on the labels, on the shop fronts. Linke, Schrapel, Langmeil, Schultz – these are the names of the people and places who define the Barossa.

Rocky O'Callaghan, one of the Barossa's legion of small, quality conscious winemakers, points out that the way the region was settled had a critical effect on the way Barossans live. It was settled in an orderly manner, with whole communities removed from the Old World to the New to escape religious persecution: the butcher, the baker, the priest all upped and shifted. And in this brave New World, everybody had an orchard, a garden,

Peter Lehmann,
Barossa legend

a well and, crucially, a small vineyard. That's a strong heritage: strong enough to sustain the Barossa through two world wars (when anyone with a German accent was treated with suspicion or hostility), and strong enough to sustain it through vine pull schemes and fluctuating tastes.

It's not just good German hard work that has made the Barossa what it is, though. This is also a great place to grow grapes and make wine. With its not-too-wet winters and warm, dry summers, it can reliably ripen high-quality grapes, year in, year out. From the warm sandy loam soils of the undulating valley floor to slightly cooler sites up in the Barossa Ranges, almost every style of wine, from heady fortified muscat to full-flavoured riesling can be – and is – produced.

Many of the country's biggest wine companies have their main wine-making operations here: Penfolds (Southcorp), Orlando, Mildara Blass and Yalumba among others crush mind-boggling quantities of grapes in the Barossa each year. And it's not just quantity that these makers value: many of them hang their quality reputation on Barossa fruit. Penfolds, for example, is perceived as a Barossa brand, even though they source fruit from all over the place. Yalumba have a strong emotional investment in the Barossa. And Orlando have taken a real creek and turned it into a worldwide brand.

It's not all big company action, either. Some of the Barossa's staunchest supporters are the medium-sized wineries like Peter Lehmann and Grant Burge, built up in the 1980s by ex big-company makers and now flourishing. And most of the Barossa's producers fall very much into the little-guy camp: growers turned maker like Kym Jenke at the Jenke winery and Peter Schulz at Turkey Flat; champions of the old, dry-grown vineyards like Rocky O'Callaghan of Rockford and Charlie Melton; and a newer breed of small makers pushing the style envelope and exploring new directions for Barossa wines, people like Rolf Binder at Veritas and David Powell at Torbreck.

The Barossa has enjoyed a particularly purple patch over the last decade. The styles of red that do well here – big, generous and concentrated

Charlie Melton,
winemaker,
Charles Melton Wines

John Vickery,
the godfather of
Australian riesling,
Richmond Grove

– are very much in demand, and the Barossa seems to be keeping up with it fairly comfortably, churning out new labels, building new wineries and coming up with new wines all the time.

As I say, a person could become addicted. Not that I am, you understand. I could give up any time. I could. Honest. Now, where was that corkscrew?

Barossa Valley flavours

Because the Barossa has done such a good PR job with its red wines over the last ten years or so, it's easy to forget that it can also make good whites – big flavoured, none too subtle, but often full of warmth and sunshine-ripe fruit. Traditionally, the Barossa white grape of choice was riesling (well, with that German heritage and all), and it is still widely planted and made. The best examples, quite broad and soft but with good floral fruit flavour, come from just above the hot valley floor itself, in the Barossa Ranges, from old family wineries like Bethany, and larger labels like Richmond Grove and Orlando, whose unique Steingarten vineyard has historically produced some great wines (although there's very little Steingarten fruit in the modern-day Steingarten wine).

There is a bit of chardonnay planted here, but it's usually made in a really warm, ripe, tropical, drink-now style. Much more successful, I reckon, is oak-aged Barossa semillon, which, from the best producers such as St Hallett, Peter Lehmann, The Willows and Heritage, makes a delicious, full-bodied, tangy, lemon and toast-flavoured wine that can age over ten years into a great complex drink.

Because most of that successful PR job has focussed on shiraz, it's also easy to forget that there are other red varieties here, too. Cabernet sauvignon has been grown in the Barossa for well over a century and, from older, low-yielding vineyards, can make some fabulously concentrated, chocolatey wines. Merlot is a more recent arrival, but seems to like the climate, making warm, round, red-fruity reds. But while I like both, I think that the flavours you get from the old grenache and mourvedre vines here are usually more exciting – the grenache is more in the tobacco, spice spectrum than, say, McLaren Vale grenache, while the mourvedre can be impressively plummy and dark. Winemakers like Charlie Melton (especially the Nine

it's hard to get away from the feeling that riesling and shiraz are still the region's top wines – even though there are relatively few shiraz wines released with 'Eden Valley' proudly splashed on the label. Standing in the magnificent Hill of Grace vineyard, surrounded by ancient old vines hunched over like gipsy grandmothers, it's impossible not to turn into an incurable old conservative, harping on about heritage and tradition and a sense of place.

Eden Valley flavours

You know how you go through binges, listening to one CD for two weeks, over and over again, or having the same dish at your favourite restaurant every time you go there? Well I get like that about wine, sometimes, and at the moment I'm on a bit of an Eden Valley riesling binge.

Eden Valley rieslings are quite different from Australia's other classic style, Clare Valley rieslings. They are much more austere, finer, floral when they're young but often ageing into more complex drinks over ten years or more in the bottle. In fact, some of the very best old Australian rieslings I've drunk have been Eden, not Clare, wines. If you were feeling internationally inclined, you could even say that Eden Valley rieslings are a little Germanic in style – indeed, the region was known as the North Rhine early in its nineteenth-century history. Pewsey Vale, Heggies and Henschke have all been making great riesling for donkey's years, as have Peter Lehmann, St Hallett and Wolf Blass – all Barossa Valley wineries using Eden fruit. The most incredible Eden rieslings of all time, though, were probably the wines made by John Vickery when he was at Leo Buring in the 1970s – legendary wines that still drink beautifully.

Of the other whites, chardonnay does very well at Mountadam's high, cool vineyard, producing wines with great richness and complexity. And Yalumba have managed to define the Australian viognier style at their Heggies vineyard: big, fat, hedonistic, creamy wines full of apricotty fruit.

Eden Valley shiraz reaches its incredibly fine, concentrated peak with Stephen and Prue Henschke's Hill of Grace and earthier, broader Mount Edelstone, but also shines in a more affordable form in wines like those

...at the moment I'm on a bit of an Eden Valley riesling binge.

from Tollana. As for the other reds, Jim Irvine has shown that merlot can be almost as concentrated, ripe and intense as shiraz, and that zinfandel in all its funky berry beauty has lots of potential. Cabernet sauvignon often finds the hard, cool conditions too much, and usually needs some merlot to flesh it out and give it weight – with exceptions, of course, such as the often plush, essencey Cyril Henschke cabernet sauvignon (low-yielding old vines shaking their thing again).

left: Stephen and Prue Henschke,
winemaker and viticulturist,
Henschke Wines

right: Adam Wynn,
vigneron,
Mountadam

Clare Valley

You won't be getting a very objective overview of the Clare Valley from me, I'm afraid. I know wine writers are meant to be fiercely independent and critical and keep their sense of detachment, but I'm not even going to bother trying.

You see, this heavenly place was where I tasted my first really exciting small producer wine – an innocent mouthful of Mitchell's Peppertree Shiraz. This altered my perception, Aldous Huxley-like, of what wine could be, and in an instant changed my life forever. I was all geared up to be an impoverished artist, starving in some loft in Paris or Berlin, astounding the art world with my ground-breaking paintings. But thanks to this taste of Clare Valley shiraz, I discovered good wine and good food, and it's all been a roly poly downhill slide ever since.

Anyway, back to the job in hand. Vineyards were first planted in the Clare Valley from the 1840s onwards, with Clare wine slaking the thirst of the thousands of miners, drovers and farmers who passed through the valley on their way to the wheat fields and silver, copper and slate mines for

the rest of that century. Many of the wineries from that period still make wine: the Jesuit-built and -run Sevenhill winery near its striking church, the old Quelltaler winery at Watervale, Birk's Wendouree tucked away behind Clare itself, and Leasingham, now owned by BRL Hardy. There are also ever-present reminders of that time in the region's solid stone buildings, its lavish pubs, and even in its ruins – old wine taverns crumbling gently in the middle of overgrown paddocks.

For the early part of the twentieth century, strong export demand for big reds and ports kept the wineries of Clare busy, so that by the time table wines became fashionable in Australia again in the 1950s and 60s, Clare's old established vineyards were well-placed to supply (the quality of fruit from these dry-grown mature vineyards is often the key to Clare's quality).

Enough of the history, though. What's happening in the Clare today? Well, the big companies are still there, in the form of Leasingham and the newer (1970s) Taylors estate. But Clare's also abuzz with activity at the medium-sized and very small level. The crazy Barry brothers at Jim Barry Wines, along with Andrew 'The Ox' Hardy at Knappstein Wines (owned by Petaluma), make large quantities of good Clare wines, while a mob of small

Adelaide Hills

Even though I hate flying, I love the descent into Adelaide. Once you've thumped down through the clouds, you approach a crumpled tapestry of orchards and vineyards at an alarming rate, getting closer and closer until you can almost touch the bunches of ripe chardonnay – and then suddenly the Hills are gone, and the suburbs of Adelaide stretch out below you towards the sea.

I love the drive up into the Hills too, the curling, twisting ascent through the Devil's Elbow, back into the clouds, it seems. It can be a bright sunny blue morning in the middle of Adelaide itself, but by the time you get up into the Hills, it can be misty and cold. You are often struck, here, by how high and detached you feel, driving up and down the region's steep folds. On top of the world, ma, on top of the world.

Another thing that strikes you about the Adelaide Hills is that it's absolutely stuffed to the gills with winemaking royalty. The list of producers reads like a veritable who's who of South Australian wine over the last twenty years: Brian Croser (the young Turk of the 1970s, wine style innovator of the 80s and wine industry politician of the 90s) at Petaluma, Geoff Weaver (ex-chief winemaker at Hardys) at his eponymous winery; Martin Shaw (ex Petaluma) and cousin Michael Hill Smith (Master of Wine, restaurateur and member of the Yalumba family) at Shaw and Smith; Tim Knappstein (ex Knappstein in the Clare Valley) at his Lenswood Vineyards; Stephen and Prue Henschke at their vineyards next to Tim Knappstein's at Lenswood; Stephen George (consultant to the fabled Wendouree in Clare) at Ashton Hills; Peter Leske (ex Australian Wine Research Institute) at Nepenthe – I mean, really, the region is bursting with impeccable credentials.

These people have got to be here for a reason. And they are: even though it's cool and wet and can be frustratingly marginal, this region – or rather, its collection of sub-regions – can produce some of the most scintillating wine in the country. Indeed, these winemakers would argue that their wines can be great *because* the Adelaide Hills are cool and wet and frustratingly marginal.

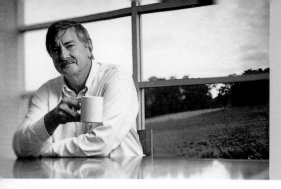

The Hills themselves were settled very soon after Adelaide itself, in the 1840s, and although the cool climate has prompted people to plant fruit trees ever since, vines and wine have been a feature of the region for only thirty years. This sense of modernity, of pioneering new flavours and styles, is one of the things, I think, that makes the region so exciting. It's certainly captured the attention of many outside the area – the much-hyped 'Yattarna' chardonnay from Penfolds, for example, is based around fruit from the Adelaide Hills, and the region is acknowledged as one of the best in the country (certainly the best in South Australia) for pinot noir and sauvignon blanc.

As I said, though, the Adelaide Hills are best understood as a collection of sub-regions. There is quite a marked difference, for example, between the very cool and wet Piccadilly in the highest part of the Hills (best for sparkling and fine chardon-nay), the slightly less cool Lenswood sub-region to the north (better for pinot noir, sauvignon blanc and even merlot), and Gumeracha and Paracombe, to the north again, up near the southern boundary of Eden Valley, where the warmer, drier con-ditions mean good ripe cabernet and shiraz.

Adelaide Hills flavours

I once had one of those great rambly lazy afternoon conversa-tions – as you do – with Peter Leske of Nepenthe. The conversation was about flavours: how we perceive them, how important they can be to us, that kind of thing (one of my jobs is to describe flavour to you, the reader, and one of Peter's jobs at the time was training people to be wine show judges, so the conversation

Michael Hill Smith,
vigneron (Shaw and Smith),
restaurateur (Universal Wine Bar)

Peter Leske,
winemaker,
Nepenthe

wasn't complete wank). We were sitting having lunch at Bridgewater Mill, one of the Adelaide Hills' great restaurants, sipping the thrillingly spicy Nepenthe zinfandel (a late-ripening grape that has no right making good wine in such a cool climate) – as you do – and I was trying to describe what I tasted in the best Hills wines. I eventually worked out that it was pure flavours – pure, crystal-clear fruit flavours.

They are there in the region's sparkling wines: Petaluma's 'Croser' can, when it's good, be one of the country's most piercingly focussed, crisp, delicate bubblies. They are there in the top pinot noirs: Lenswood Vineyards, Ashton Hills and Hillstowe all make wines with brooding dark cherries and depth. Those crystal-clear flavours are most certainly there in the best chardonnays, too: Petaluma and Geoff Weaver make beautiful, subtle, elegant wines, creamy at the edges but with this core of startling nectarine-like fruit. And they sing in the sauvignon blancs: Shaw and Smith, Lenswood Vineyards and Geoff Weaver make three of the best examples in the country, with sometimes embarrassingly pungent blackcurrant and passionfruit flavours and heaps of life and zest.

These are the region's high-profile wines, but there are others that also display such clarity. In the northern part, the shiraz cabernet from Paracombe and the cabernet merlot from Chain of Ponds both have wonderful intensity and dark black fruits. At Lenswood, Tim Knappstein and the Henschkes both make exceptional, surprisingly ripe tightly structured blends of merlot and cabernet, while Nepenthe and Geoff Weaver switch the varieties around and make slightly leaner, lighter, leafier wines (a little too leafy for some, perhaps).

Riesling, though, is the most underrated variety. From top producers like Ashton Hills, Henschke and Weaver, Adelaide hills riesling can vie with Eden Valley in its delicate, crisp, zesty austerity.

McLaren Vale

Somehow, every time I find myself in McLaren Vale I end up eating and drinking stupidly well. Like the Barossa, this region just to the south of Adelaide has developed a strong tucker culture, embracing its distinctly Mediterranean climate and giving it a big, hungry, wine-stained kiss.

Part of that culture was established in the 1840s and 50s by the region's first English settlers, who were so taken with the 'continental' feel of the place that they planted almond and olive groves alongside their vineyards. Much of it was built up by the local Italian community who became big grape growers in the twentieth century. And the gaps have been filled in during the last few decades by third- and fourth-generation winemakers, a new wave of 1970s boutique vignerons and local restaurateurs.

These guys have either injected a touch of exotica or promoted what was already there: people like Mark Lloyd of Coriole vineyard, who championed olives and olive oil; Russell Jeavons, renegade chef who brought Asian influences and the district's renowned wood-fired pizza oven; and Pip Forrester of the Salopian Inn restaurant, one of the first to serve dukkah, the Middle Eastern spice and nut mix that goes so well with the region's olive oil and crusty bread (and sparkling reds).

McLaren Vale reached a peak at the beginning of the twentieth century, thanks to its thriving trade with England (mostly heavy port and big 'burgundies'), while a healthy trade in providing wine for big Australian companies – such as the McLaren Vale-based Hardys – kept the region busy as the century wore on. The region's warmth and deep rich soils, tempered by the ever-present sea breezes could – and can – produce red wines with middle-of-the-tongue plumpness, perfect for blending with leaner wines from cooler climates.

Having said that, in the old days these red wines could also sometimes have distinctly 'ferruginous' earthy flavours. They could also be fairly stinky, barn-yardy wines that tended to pack a punch. Not terribly modern, in other words.

Over the last decade or so, though, McLaren Vale has redefined itself. Like a Californian Baby Boomer, it has gone into some deep rebirthing

Steve Pannell, chief red winemaker, Hardys

therapy and come out the other side much cleaner, much purer, much more well-groomed. The wines are better, arguably, then they have ever been, and McLaren Vale shiraz in particular is the flavour of the month with wine shows, competitions and critics around the world (particularly in the United States). There is also the right mix of the big (with Hardys, Seaview – now called Edwards and Chaffey – and Normans dominating), and the little (Clarendon Hills' limited releases of hyper-expensive single-vineyard wines), the old (d'Arenberg, Kay's Amery) and the new (the resurrected Tatachilla, the hugely cult-like Fox Creek), and the staunchly traditional (Pirramimma and Woodstock) and the progressive (Noon's ultra-ripe reds, Kangarilla Road's zinfandel). It's a mix that really works, and makes this one of the best places in Australia to visit.

In fact, the McLaren Vale winemakers are now one of the most organised, publicity hungry mobs in the whole industry, successfully promoting the region's show successes, food culture and festivals (the Continuous Picnic, the Sea and Vines festival, the crowning of the Bushing King festival among others). The recently completed McLaren Vale Visitor's Centre – a tasting room, function room, cafe, information service, all rolled into one – is the kind of venue it would be great to see every wine region have.

McLaren Vale flavours

Sweet. It's a fairly simple word, you would have thought. But in wine tasting language, it doesn't always mean sugary. Sometimes, the word sweet can refer to a generosity of fruit flavour that gives the impression of sweetness on your tongue but doesn't actually involve sugar. A wine that has been matured in bold-flavoured new American oak can also smell sweet. I find myself using the word sweet a lot when I'm tasting McLaren Vale wines.

The white wines in this part of the world are good but they aren't, on the whole, as exciting as the reds. There are exceptions: chardonnay, particularly from the cooler parts of the Vale, moving up into the Adelaide Hills, can be deliciously sweet (there's that word) and full of melon fruit; semillon, from good producers such as Coriole, can be citrussy and toasty, in similar fashion to the Barossa semillon; and verdelho, chenin blanc and sauvignon blanc can be attractive, in a full, tropical style (Coriole again, Chapel Hill and Fox Creek are names to look for).

The reds, on the other hand, can be every bit as exciting as their reputation would suggest. I recently spent a day tasting my way through five vintages of eighteen of McLaren Vale's top shirazes. It was one of the most enjoyable tastings I've ever done: the sheer voluptuousness and richness of the some of the wines – the sheer sexiness, if you want to be blunt – made me giddy with pleasure. Each of the producers sources fruit from different parts of the Vale, and they each have a different approach to making – some, like Wirra Wirra, going easy on the oak, using older barrels; some, like Hardys and Tatachilla, going in hard on the oak but using predominantly French; and some, like Fox Creek and Rosemount's huge 'Balmoral' wine, going hell-for-leather down the full-on new, sweet American oak route. But underlying all of them is this rich, bramble, blackberry jam, chocolate flavour. Yum, yum, yum.

McLaren Vale cabernet has often shared some of that sweet black fruit over the years, with Seaview (now Edwards and Chaffey), Chapel Hill, Normans Chais Clarendon, Chateau Reynella and Shottesbrooke leading the way. More recently, the earlier-ripening and cuddlier merlot has arrived with a soft splash, seeming to be even more suited to the Vale's inherent softness, producing some fabulously opulent wines from wineries like Tatachilla and Clarendon Hills.

Which leaves grenache and mourvedre. There are, as in the Barossa, some priceless old, dry-grown vineyards of these varieties here, and over the last ten years, McLaren Vale has run parallel to the Barossa in the race to put them back on the map. Today it is home to some startlingly good wines: richer than the Barossa wines, softer, rounder. The standouts for me are the sensational earth wines from d'Arenberg, and the ultra-ripe, luscious, strong black wines from Drew Noon.

d'Arry Osborn and Chester Osborn, vignerons, d'Arenberg Wines

Langhorne Creek

While McLaren Vale has strutted around centre stage in the spotlight for well over a hundred years, poor old Langhorne Creek, about fifty kilometres to the east, near Lake Alexandrina, has spent most of that time up the back, in the chorus.

Vines were planted here as long ago as 1860, when Frank Potts established the Bleasdale winery, named in honour of the Reverend Joseph Ignatius Bleasdale, Melbourne's nineteenth-century Len Evans. More importantly, vines have grown here continuously since that period, with Bleasdale still producing and some of the huge old shiraz plants in the Metala vineyard well past their hundredth birthday and showing no signs of slowing down.

This is flat, warm country, traditionally irrigated by diverting water from the River Bremer or the lake, and the wine it produces is among the ripest, softest and most relaxed in the country – like McLaren Vale on opium. Big companies such as Wolf Blass, Orlando, Saltram and others have known this for decades, and have often used Langhorne Creek wine to fill out a blend, to add approachability and softness to their wines. But the name features on the label – with the honourable exception of the famous Stonyfell Metala shiraz cabernet (now owned by Mildara Blass).

This low profile isn't surprising when you consider there are only four wineries here – three of which were established in the 1980s – and it does not have quite the same bustling tourist appeal as McLaren Vale or the Adelaide Hills. But it's a low profile that may not last forever: the landscape has gone seriously stripey over the last decade, with huge vineyards cropping up all over the place, vine row after vine row marching across the flatlands in regimented order. While most of the fruit from these vineyards is being used anonymously in big brands such as Jacob's Creek, it's a fairly safe bet that some will start appearing in wines that have the name Langhorne Creek proudly splashed across the label.

RED GUM LEVER PRESS
DIMENSIONS
HEIGHT — 23 FEET
LENGTH — 43 FEET
WEIGHT OF LEVER — 32 TONS
CAGE CAPACITY — 25 ½ TONS
BUILT IN 1892 USED UNTIL 1962

Langhorne Creek flavours

Single varietal wines that do well here include ripe, tropical verdelho from Bleasdale, apple-saucy chenin blanc from Temple Bruer, vibrantly plummy malbec from Bleasdale and seriously rich shiraz from everybody (especially the limited release original vineyard Metala shiraz). But the red blends are, for me, the wines that hold the most interest: the 'standard' Metala, of course, a model for Australian shiraz cabernet; Temple Bruer's spicy shiraz malbec; Bleasdale's big, complex 'Frank Potts' cabernet malbec merlot; and Lake Breeze's impressively dense, round cabernet shiraz.

Michael Potts,
tired winemaker,
Bleasdale

Coonawarra

You've always got to be a little sceptical of big reputations. Sometimes, the hype surrounding a wine or a region can be so huge that it outweighs the actual quality. Sometimes the hype can be so well entrenched that people don't realise – or are unwilling to admit – that quality isn't living up to expectations.

Coonawarra is perhaps Australia's most hyped region. Ever since the 1950s, when David Wynn's newly acquired Wynns Coonawarra Estate burst onto the market with its seriously stylish wines and their seriously stylish labels, Coonawarra has been referred to as Australia's leading producer of fine red wines.

So, is it? For the last few years, I would have said, well, probably not. A few less-than-great vintages producing some rather weak, thin, green wines, political squabbling over the boundaries of the Coonawarra GI, and the huge success of big reds from warmer climates (the Barossa, McLaren Vale) or cabernets from other areas (Margaret River) all cast a shadow over Coonawarra's reputation – in my mind at least. But in 1999, I changed my mind.

First, I was privileged to taste the famous Woodley 'Treasure Chest' series of Coonawarra wines from the late 1940s and early 50s. These wines have a reputation that borders on the religious. They are the kind of wines that inspired most of the winemakers who have flocked to Coonawarra since the 1960s. These Woodleys were made from fifty-year-old shiraz vines by Bill Redman, then virtually Coonawarra's sole winemaker (the region was fleetingly developed as a wine district by John Riddoch in the 1890s, but never took off – too remote, too cool, too bloody hard). I was expecting to be disappointed by these old wines – they couldn't possibly be as good as everybody made them out to be – but I was absolutely floored by their extraordinary finesse, purity of berry fruit flavour and sheer liveliness – especially the 1949!

Yeah, I know, a wine writer carping on yet again about wines you'll never get to taste. Well you'll be pleased to know that my second big Coonawarra wine conversion from 1999 was tasting some barrel samples of the region's best cabernet sauvignons made in 1998 – wines, in other words, that you may very well be able to buy. These were as staggering in

their boldness as the Woodleys were ethereal: thrillingly vibrant, purple, intense, tongue-hugging, life-affirming wines.

So is Coonawarra the greatest red wine region in Australia? Weeeell … possibly. It certainly makes some of the best cabernet in the country. But *the* best?

The first time I went to Coonawarra, I'm not ashamed to say that I jumped out of the car and bent down to kiss the famous glowing red soil. Everybody talks about this soil – the terra rossa, weathered red earth over limestone, so perfect for growing grapes. What they don't talk about so much is the fact that not all the thousands of hectares of vineyards down here are on this hallowed terra rossa turf. Indeed, many are on the rather less inspiring, Christmas cake-like black soils and sandy loams that surround the cigar-shaped strip of terra rossa.

All of which has led to some pretty bitter arguments. Do the terra rossa soils make that much of a difference, or is Coonawarra's cool climate more of a defining factor? Should Brian Croser be allowed to label his cabernet as Coonawarra when most of the grapes for the wine come from a vineyard just north of the regional boundary?

Luckily, this last one's been resolved (at least it had when I wrote these words), and Croser's vineyard has been allowed to join the gang. But other philosophical differences still exist, particularly those between the small, family-owned producers like Bowen Estate and the bigger boys like Wynns and Lindemans: arguments between those who hand prune and pick their vineyards and those who use machines; arguments over what type of oak Coonawarra cabernet should be aged in (sweeter American, or more savoury French); arguments over adding tannin to fermenting red wines to give them more oomph than the climate naturally produces.

Of course, these arguments wouldn't be so heated if there wasn't so much at stake: after all, Coonawarra is Australia's greatest red wine region. Isn't it?

...after all, Coonawarra is Australia's greatest red wine region. Isn't it?

Doug Bowen,
winemaker,
Bowen Estate

Coonawarra flavours

Cabernet, cabernet, cabernet. The way people go on about Coonawarra being the best region in the entire universe for cabernet sauvignon, you'd be forgiven for thinking that cabernet was all they grew down here. It's true, they do grow a lot (and so would you, if you knew it was the best region, etc.), but they grow other stuff, too.

They grow riesling, for example, and people like Wynns turn it into really attractive, sweetly floral, juicy white wine. And sauvignon blanc, in an often quite pungent fashion, as at Katnook Estate. They grow chardonnay, too, and Balnaves, Punters Corner and Wynns again have made lovely, toasty crisp wines. I'm also going to mention pinot noir, even though I've rarely had one from here that I've liked (Rouge Homme being a notable good-value exception).

Bearing in mind Coonawarra's huge cabernet reputation, it comes as a surprise to learn that shiraz was what most of the early, classic Coonawarra reds were made from. Shiraz is nowhere near as widely planted as cabernet today, but it can (especially in warmer years) make great wine: Wynns, Bowen Estate, Zema, Rymill, Brand's, Majella all do well with it in a vivid purple, black peppery, medium-bodied style (Wynns Michael is from older vines and is matured in lashings of American oak, so is much fuller bodied). Majella and Penley Estate also make good cabernet–shiraz blends.

Merlot is the next big thing, according to every winemaker who's got some planted, and the few varietal wines to have emerged from Coonawarra (Petaluma, Katnook Estate) seem to bear this out with their cedary, herbal-edged intensity. Most of the merlot, though is used in blends with cabernet.

Ah, yes, cabernet. Did I mention that Coonawarra is considered to be the greatest … I did? Well let me tell you why. At its best, from producers like Wynns, Bowen Estate, Parker, Petaluma, Penley and Katnook, Coonawarra cabernet has this totally seductive smell and flavour of crushed mulberries and blackcurrants, and this combination of concentration and elegance in the mouth and this ability to age into the most incredible, cedary, ethereal, complex … all right, enough already. I think you've got the picture.

The Limestone Coast

One of the other reasons why Coonawarra lost a bit of its shine in the 1990s is that it suddenly had challengers to its title clambering over the back fence. Immediately to the north around the hamlet of Koppamurra, to the south near Mount Gambier, and over on the coast, near Robe and Mount Benson, vineyards started appearing, all claiming to share a little of Coonawarra's specialness – its magic terra rossa. Suddenly, the game was up: Coonawarra wasn't unique after all, merely one of many potential regions, some of which may even produce better wine.

Ralph Fowler, then winemaker at Leconfield and now winemaker for himself (and a couple of others) once pulled out a geological map of South Australia's south-east and pointed to Coonawarra's low ridge of limestone, formed as the sea receded over the millennia. Then he pointed out all the other ridges that exist in that part of the world, and it suddenly came into focus. Imagine, he said, a Limestone Coast super blend, with cabernet from Koppamurra, merlot from Coonawarra, and cabernet franc and petit verdot from Mount Benson. So imagine I did, and boy, it tasted good.

Padthaway, about 100 kilometres north of Coonawarra, was the first of the Limestone Coast regions to be established, first by Seppelt and then by Hardys, Lindemans and Orlando, along with other independent grape growers. The point to remember is that the region was developed from the start as a fruit factory: until 1998, when Hardys finished their huge Stonehaven facility, there was only one winery, Padthaway Estate, and the vast majority of grapes grown in the district were (and are) trucked out. You'll find the Padthaway name on a few labels from the big (and not so big companies), but most of the time you'll be drinking wine with Padthaway fruit in it and you won't know it.

Wrattonbully, just to the north of Coonawarra, has experienced a huge vineyard explosion over the last ten years (it was originally called Koppamurra, but one of the region's first vineyards, Koppamurra Wines, objected to the big companies nicking its mellifluous moniker, and dug its intellectual property heels in – hence the rather silly W word compromise). This is the big one: hundreds and hundreds of hectares of mostly red grape vines planted by big companies like Yalumba and Mildara Blass, all just beginning to produce serious quantities of fruit. A lot of people are predicting huge things from Wrattonbully's warmer, undulating terra rossa vineyards – some are even daring to suggest it could topple Coonawarra's red wine crown.

In contrast, Mount Benson and Robe, right over on the coast, are cooler than Coonawarra, due mostly to the winds that whistle in from the sea. Early wines from Cape Jaffa and a vineyard established by Rhone Valley winemakers Chapoutier have been encouragingly fine, elegant and intense. And south of Coonawarra, a few growers are pushing the boundaries further by experimenting in the even cooler Mount Gambier region.

Limestone Coast flavours

One minute I think Padthaway is white wine country, when I taste one of the crunchy, citrussy Hardys chardonnays or excellent tangeriney Lindemans botrytis rieslings or grassy sauvignon blancs. The next minute I'm convinced it's great for reds, either as good value pinot noirs (Lindemans again) or elegant, Coonawarra-ish cabernets (Hardys again), or surprisingly gutsy, intense shiraz (Hardys or Orlando 'Lawson's').

It's a bit too soon to tell what will eventually do best in Wrattonbully and Mount Benson, but early predictions about cabernet and merlot – warmer, rounder, fuller in the former, leaner, more poised in the latter – look to be holding true. Again, not too many wines proclaim Wrattonbully proudly on the label – yet.

Victoria

Victorian Wine Regions

1   Far South-West
2   The Grampians
3   Pyrenees
4   Ballarat
5   Geelong
6   Bendigo and Heathcote
7   Macedon Ranges
8   Sunbury
9   Mornington Peninsula
10 Yarra Valley
11 The High Country
12 Goulburn Valley
13 Glenrowan
14 Rutherglen
15 North-East Victoria
16 Gippsland

All right. I admit it. I'm hopelessly biased when it comes to Victorian wine. I live, after all, in Melbourne, surrounded by some of the best cooler climate regions in Australia. I can hop in the car and within an hour be right in the thick of it: standing in a freezing cold cellar in the Macedon Ranges, waiting with glass outstretched as a winemaker disgorges a bottle of crisp, apple-and-bread-dough-flavoured bubbly; breathing in the history of one of the Yarra Valley's century-old winery buildings, tasting bright purple young cabernet straight out of the barrel and feeling it vibrate on my tongue; sitting in the sun on top of Red Hill on the Mornington Peninsula, looking out across the wide blue bay, washing a pile of local mussels down with gulp after gulp of honey and peach-flavoured chardonnay …

And if I decide to keep driving, up and over the Great Dividing Range to the north, or out through the interminable flat, parched country of the Western Districts, I move into different climates and different experiences: lapping up the smells of brazil nuts and bat shit in a 120-year-old muscat cellar in Rutherglen, watching as Bill Chambers slowly draws dark, treacly liquid from an ancient cask; jumping half naked into a deep vat of seething shiraz skins in a half-finished winery in Heathcote; munching on spring lamb and sipping elegant cabernet in the far south-west corner of the state.

The point is that Victoria may not be the largest producing wine state in the country – South Australia holds that position, thanks to seriously big regions like the Riverland – but it's definitely the most diverse.

The Yarra Valley has been a very noisy place of late. Since the beginning of the 1990s, its wide blue hills and dusty gum forests have echoed with the thump of vineyard strainer posts being knocked into the ground, the grind of cranes and earth movers clearing more space for glamorous new wineries, the clamour of machine harvesters edging their way along endless vine rows, and the chatter of wine writers welcoming the Yarra's renaissance (with me chattering as loudly as the rest of them). In the 1880s, this was Victoria's leading wine region. Now it is again.

Yarra Valley

(You're going to get sick of hearing this refrain by the time you've got to the end of these chapters on Victoria by the way – you know, region finds wine, region loses wine, region finds wine again – but it really is a story common to most of them.)

In the Yarra Valley's case, the story starts in 1838, when the Ryrie brothers travelled overland from New South Wales and stuck a few vines in the ground at Yering, north-east of Melbourne – then a muddy three-year-old village at the mouth of the Yarra River. The story picks up when a group of upper-crust Swiss settlers bought big tracts of land in the district, and, encouraged by some good, Burgundy-like wine made from the Ryries' original vineyard, decided to plant some vines themselves.

By the 1880s, the story reached its first climax, with Paul de Castella's Yering vineyard, his brother Hubert de Castella's St Huberts estate, and Guill de Pury's Yeringberg all boasting substantial vineyards and extravagant wineries, and all winning gongs for their wines all over the world.

By the 1920s, though, these glam vineyards had all gone. The Australian public weren't all that interested in light, European-style wines at the time, and all the export market wanted was big, heavy red and port. So, for forty years, the only signs of wine culture in the valley were a couple of wine saloons in the town of Lilydale, and some crumbling deserted cellars.

From the 1960s on, though, the wine returned, in three distinct waves. First, there were the pioneers: people like Bailey Carrodus at Yarra Yering and John Middleton at Mount Mary. Second, a big influx of smaller players, inspired by the pioneers' early efforts: people like David and Cathy Lance at

Diamond Valley, David and Christine Fyffe down at Yarra Burn, moving up a notch in the 1980s when people like Louis Bialkower established Yarra Ridge and James Halliday planted Coldstream Hills.

It's the third, noisy wave that has brought the Yarra back some of its nineteenth-century grandeur, though. Since the late 1980s, the big companies have moved into the region – De Bortoli buying Graeme Miller's Chateau Yarrinya, the French champagne house Moët and Chandon establishing their Green Point vineyards to produce Domaine Chandon fizz, and then, in the 1990s, BRL Hardy buying Yarra Burn, McWilliam's buying Lillydale Vineyards, Mildara Blass buying Yarra Ridge and Southcorp buying Coldstream Hills. There's money, not water, flowing through the Yarra Valley these days – and all three of the region's original grand wineries are making wine again, not perhaps in exactly the same spots, but mostly in the same spirit.

A huge endorsement from the biggest wine companies in Australia was bound to lead to an influx of other investors in the Yarra Valley – and that's precisely what's happened. Every time I drive out to the region I come across a new vineyard, or another cellar door, or a big paddock being cleared for vines.

Wonderful as the history of the Yarra is, though, and much as I love wandering through the incredible Chateau Yering homestead (Paul de Castella's original house and now a luxury small hotel), trying to imagine the de Castellas sipping their wine after an autumn morning's hunting, it's not what attracts the big companies here. What they're more concerned with is the Yarra's ability to produce great booze.

There are distinct sub-regions within the Yarra Valley: the warmer, northern vineyards around De Bortoli, the slightly cooler middle vineyards on the grey loamy soils of the area around Coldstream, and the much cooler vineyards right down south, in the red volcanic hills around Seville. Each of these sub-regions produces wines with different flavours, but at their best, they all share a magic combination of intensity and finesse.

Yarra Valley flavours

Forget the word 'big'. It just doesn't enter into a discussion of the wines of the Yarra Valley. Even with the most concentrated, intense, flavoursome

cabernets and shirazes to have come from the region – Yarra Yering's amazing Dry Reds No. 1 and No. 2 or the reserve reds Rob Dolan made when he was at Yarra Ridge – and even in a low-yielding drought vintage like 1997, there's always an elegance, a poise to the wines of the Yarra that is the opposite of bigness.

Chardonnay is the Yarra Valley's top white, producing lovely white peach and citrus-flavoured wines, often complexed by toasty new oak flavours and a nutty creaminess from malolactic fermentation – Coldstream Hills, De Bortoli and TarraWarra are best for a fuller example,

left: Wayne Donaldson,
winemaker, Domaine Chandon

right: Clare Halloran,
winemaker, TarraWarra Estate

hordes of mates who'd drive down to help them pick and prune were soon treated to a healthy dose of reality, though, because, like all potentially great cool-climate wine regions, the Peninsula can be marginal grape-growing country.

Frosts can be a problem; rain often brings moulds and mildews; the autumn can dribble into winter before all the grapes are ripe; and the fertile volcanic soils of Red Hill (where many of the most romantic vineyard

above: Kathleen Quealy,
Kevin McCarthy (and family),
T'Gallant Winemakers

right: Garry Crittenden,
winemaker, Dromana Estate

sites were chosen) can, if you're not careful, turn a vine into a huge fruit-producing monster – and large crops are the last thing you want if you're trying to ripen your grapes in a cold year.

Not that these hardships stemmed the wave of wannabe vignerons, though, and there are two good reasons for this. Firstly, when the right site has been chosen and the vines have been well managed – and, importantly, when the season is kind – the Peninsula can produce great grapes. And great grapes, if they're handled properly, can produce great wine.

Secondly, the Mornington Peninsula is still Melbourne's playground, with increasing tourism from interstate and overseas. All of which translates into that magic phrase 'cellar door sales'. I reckon there are more cellar doors per square kilometre crammed into this narrow strip of land jutting into Bass Strait than in any other wine region in Australia.

For many years, there were only half a dozen or so full-time, professional winemakers on the Peninsula: people like Tod Dexter at Stoniers (now part-owned by the South Australian-based company Petaluma), Kevin McCarthy and Kathleen Quealy at T'Gallant (who make wines for other vineyards as well as their own), Jenny Bright (ex-Red Hill), and Garry Crittenden at Dromana Estate.

I reckon there are more cellar doors per square kilometre crammed into this narrow strip of land jutting into Bass Strait than in any other wine region in Australia.

But the last ten years have seen some of the weekend vignerons give up their weekday jobs and get stuck into their wineries (Lindsay McCall at Paringa Estate), grape growers build wineries and start their own label (David Leslie at Turramurra Estate) and existing wineries add restaurants (Willow Creek) – all really encouraging developments. The last five years have also seen some seriously big vineyards being planted – 100 hectares here, 50 hectares there …

Add a couple of abnormally warm vintages (resulting in perhaps misleadingly ripe wines) and that wave of wannabe vignerons looks like turning into a bit of a tsunami.

I find Mornington Peninsula wines some of the most distinctive in the country. There is a great diversity of soil types and micro climates, and even more diverse approaches to winemaking, all of which produce nuances of flavour. But I find that the prevailing maritime influence (a Peninsula, after all, is a body of land surrounded by water) usually casts a regional shadow over those subtleties. So, even if you compare a pale pinot noir grown in the coolest volcanic soils of Red Hill and made with no new oak with a darker pinot grown in the sandier loams of Dromana and made using lashings of new oak, I still think they share an underlying Mornington Peninsula-ness.

That regional character expresses itself in different ways in different varieties, of course. The early-ripening grapes pinot noir and chardonnay are the region's top varieties, with pinot often showing a spicy, bush-litter, sometimes stalky edge that becomes really complex with bottle age, and chardonnay often showing a core of rich, honeyed peachy fruit, even if the wine overall is quite crisp and lean. Both wines are often made more complex by oak handling – new oak adding a smoky layer to the pinot and a creaminess to the chardonnay – and chardonnay is also allowed to run around in the nude, with T'Gallant being early advocates of the unwooded style in the 1990s.

Among the other whites, pinot gris, again championed by T'Gallant, shows the most promise, again with a core of honey fruit, regardless of whether the wine is a lighter, pinot grigio style or a heavier, pinot gris style. Sauvignon blanc, riesling and even more exotic varieties like viognier and marsanne are also grown but seldom match the quality of chardonnay and pinot gris.

Shiraz can be successful here – surprisingly, given that shiraz is essentially a warm-climate grape and this is essentially a cool climate. Its success is very site-specific, though, and the intensely peppery, taut wines from warm vineyards like Paringa Estate and Merricks are one-offs, not easily replicated right across the Peninsula. Likewise, the late-ripening cabernet sauvignon can occasionally do well, producing intensely blackcurrant, elegant wines, but only in the warmer spots and the warmer vintages, and often when it's blended with merlot as it is at Dromana Estate.

Geelong

I have a big vested interest in Geelong. No, I don't own a vineyard down there, and no, I'm not employed by any of the wineries to write nice things about them. It's a much more selfish interest than that, and has a lot to do with me wanting to enjoy myself as much as possible.

You see, for the last few years I've been one of three judges involved in the Geelong Wine Show. This is not a glamorous affair involving getting dressed up in a white coat and scribbling reverentially on a clipboard, followed by a black-tie dinner and speeches from the mayor. It's more about sitting around in a room for a couple of hours and choosing the best wines from a narrow field, then going out to lunch. After all, in the first year we only had fourteen entries; in the second year that had more than doubled to over thirty – all of which should give you some indication of how few wineries there are in the region. The point is that I want these few wineries to do the best they can with their grapes so that my task as a judge can be as enjoyable as possible – oh, and so that you get to drink better wine, too.

There's no doubt that Geelong, with its strongly maritime climate and relatively low rainfall, can produce great grapes. The huge community of mainly Swiss vine growers that settled here in the 1850s and 60s obviously knew it: they established vineyards all around the emerging city, and, by all accounts, produced top booze. At its height, Geelong was a wine region on a par with the Yarra Valley, in both size and reputation, which made it one of the largest and most important in Australia. But then in the 1870s, as I've already described elsewhere in this book, Geelong was devastated by the terrible vine louse, phylloxera – or rather, it was destroyed by a government which took drastic measures to eradicate the louse and ended up destroying the industry.

Finally, in the 1960s, after almost a century of drought, the wine began to flow again. Daryl Sefton, a descendent of one of the region's first vignerons, and his wife Nini established the Idyll vineyard just outside Geelong in 1966. They were followed in the 1970s by a succession of small vineyards such as the now-famous Bannockburn. And, in a nice, neat

circle, the Prince Albert vineyard just south of the city was replanted a couple of years later.

During the 1980s, the Geelong wine region spread out further than it had done in the nineteenth century, when David and Vivienne Browne planted Scotchman's Hill Vineyard on the black volcanic soils of the Bellarine Peninsula, jutting out into Port Phillip Bay across from the Mornington Peninsula. Today, though, few other wineries have joined the core that had been established by the beginning of the 90s; vineyards are constantly being planted, but mostly to sell fruit to the existing wineries. Geelong seems to be stubbornly refusing to relive the vast glories of its past.

Taste the best Geelong wines and you wonder why. At their peak, from winemakers such as Gary Farr at Bannockburn and Robin Brockett at Scotchman's Hill, they are equal to the wines of the other cool regions surrounding Melbourne. Perhaps Geelong has simply been overlooked in favour of the Yarra (more available land), and Mornington (closer to all the holiday houses, meaning more cellar door trade). If so, then the only way the region will attract more attention is by churning out more great wines. And if the last two years of the Geelong Wine Show are any indication, this is precisely what's beginning to happen.

Gary Farr, winemaker, Bannockburn Vineyard

Geelong flavours

You really feel the proximity of the water in Geelong: getting stuck into some simple grilled whiting in a restaurant looking out across Corio Bay, or tucking into a big bowl of mussels down at Queenscliff on the Bellarine Peninsula, you feel like the rumble of the surf is always lurking as a constant background noise. Luckily, there's lots of good Geelong white wine to wash down your seafood with: not-too-pungent sauvignon blanc with an underlying steeliness; similarly austere riesling; citrussy, tangy chardonnay and even the odd bottle or two of savoury pinot gris.

Pinot noir is the leading red grape variety – by reputation, if not hectares planted. Whether it's Bannockburn's dense, sturdy, complex expression of the grape, or the perfumed, bright cherry fruit in the wine from Prince Albert, there is an underlying fullness and grip to Geelong pinot that sets it apart from other Victorian regions' pinot. Cabernet can do well here in a fairly tannic, slightly minty, grippy style, especially in those vineyards situated away from the coast, and especially in a blend – with merlot (as at Scotchman's Hill) or malbec (as at the small Mount Duneed winery just off the arrow-straight Surf Coast Highway). There's a fair bit of shiraz down here, too, in two distinct styles: rich, warm, earthy wines from mature vineyards such as Idyll and Tarcoola, and bursting with bright pepper and spice from Bannockburn.

One of the most memorable meals I've had involved Geelong wine – Bannockburn pinot noir, in fact. It was a lunch in a little fibro cottage in the middle of one of Bannockburn's original vineyards, drinking Gary Farr's superb pinot from his special close-planted vineyard out of fine Riedel glasses, and eating frankfurters wrapped in sliced white bread, drizzled with ketchup. It's not, perhaps, a combination that everybody's going to want to try at home, but at the time, it was bloody magnificent.

Sunbury

For years and years, the vineyards of Sunbury, immediately to the north of Melbourne, were lumped in with their neighbours in the Macedon Ranges, immediately to the north again. Macedon and Sunbury, the region was loosely called, even though everybody knew this was a little odd: after all, you only had to drive up the highway to see how different the lower, dry plains of Sunbury are to the high, wet, granite country of the Ranges. You only had to taste the wines produced in each part of the world to realise that the climates are equally different: Sunbury's wines are riper, fuller (but still elegant), while those produced in the Macedon Ranges are finer, cooler.

The problem was that there simply weren't enough wineries in Sunbury to make the break: to apply for a Geographical Indication, you need at least five vineyards of five hectares each, and the region needs to produce in total at least 500 tonnes of grapes. And it wasn't until the late 1990s that this happened.

Sunbury can now stand tall as a region in its own right, stretching from Bulla, just north of Melbourne Airport, round in an arc to Melton, north-west of the city. It's not the first time Sunbury has stood tall: it was a well-known source of good grog in the nineteenth century, when the big bluestone wineries Goona Warra and Craiglee, established by a couple of politicians, James Goodall and James Johnstone in the 1860s, were in full production. Like so many other Victorian regions, it ran out of steam early in the twentieth century, but the bluestone buildings remain and, since the 1970s revival, are once again used as wine cellars.

Craiglee was the first vineyard I visited when I moved to Melbourne almost ten years ago. I took a train one cold winter's morning from the city out to Sunbury and walked to the winery (which, I soon found out, is

There, inside the dusty bluestone cellars, as pale winter sunlight crept in through the thick glass of a small window, I tasted Pat Carmody's legendary elegant peppery shiraz and all my preconceptions about Australia as the brash New World wine country were shattered in one fell swoop.

further than you think when you look at it on a map). There, inside the dusty bluestone cellars, as pale winter sunlight crept in through the thick glass of a small window, I tasted Pat Carmody's legendary elegant peppery shiraz and all my preconceptions about Australia as the brash New World wine country were shattered in one fell swoop.

Here was a quiet winery, stuffed with history, and a quiet winemaker, quietly producing wines with far more similarity to European styles than 'Australian' styles. I'm going to like it here, I thought at the time. And I have.

Sunbury flavours

Now just because Sunbury is warmer than the Macedon Ranges doesn't make it a warm-climate region. Far from it: we're still south of the Great Divide, where the winds can be chill and the frosts severe, and in the really cool years the grapes can struggle to ripen.

Shiraz is perceived as the regional speciality, even though it is only produced really well by Craiglee. At its best it has great white pepper spiciness, backed up by dark, ripe cherry fruit and a fine, tight, medium-bodied intensity. Far more pinot noir is grown here, and I was a little sceptical about whether it was right for the region until relatively new winery Ray-Monde began producing some lovely wines – again with good dark berry fruit. Many people grow cabernet sauvignon, with the most successful examples coming from Wildwood in the south of the region, and Goona Warra, just across the road from Craiglee, has done well with lively, lighter-bodied cabernet franc.

Chardonnay is the best white, producing wines in a good, fine, citrussy style, while small batches again of semillon (Goona Warra) and viognier (Wildwood) have been produced.

Macedon Ranges

Why on earth would you bother growing grapes in the Macedon Ranges? It's a cold place, for a start, with many of the vineyards tucked away behind granite outcrops, sheltering from the wind, or perched precariously on hillsides up to 900 metres above sea level, overlooking dense bushland. Grapes can ripen late here: when the last languid rays of autumn see the last languid grapes plucked from vines everywhere else in the country, the vignerons of Macedon are rugged up like Yorkshire shepherds waiting for theirs to ripen, Mr 'erriot. And it can be wet, too, with icy rain slicing through your clothes as you're pruning, or falling as persistent drizzle in early spring.

The answer, of course, is simple (if a little perplexing to anybody not bitten by the wine bug): you bother growing grapes in the Macedon Ranges because if you find the right, sun-exposed site, and the weather is kind, and you get your grapes ripe, you can make fantastic wine. And enough people have (found the right spot and been lucky with the seasons) to cement the region's reputation.

The first man crazy enough to plant vines here was Melbourne restaurateur and all-round character Tom Lazar, at Virgin Hills, near Kyneton, in 1968. He planted cabernet and shiraz, mainly, but soon learned that the harsh climate was seldom kind: only one year in four is the vintage warm enough to take Virgin Hills beyond a light, slightly green wine into the realms of dark, intense, damson plum and spice-filled greatness.

This early pioneering work and the success the Knight family had with riesling and shiraz at their (ever-so-slightly) warmer site further west encouraged others. These newcomers, though, were more realistic and most planted the more appropriate, early-ripening chardonnay and pinot noir grapes. Which is the best thing that could have happened to the region, because these two varieties are the building blocks for great sparkling wine – a wine style that flourishes in cold climates.

Today, while some excellent table wines are produced, it's definitely the sparklings that shine. Producers such as Hanging Rock, Cleveland and Cope Williams have made fizz their flagship style, and do very well indeed. It's still mostly small, family-operated winery stuff, though. With the

All the region needs now is a big company to invest heavily – preferably a French champagne house – and the whole world will know about Macedon.

exception of John and Ann Ellis at Hanging Rock, who produce lots of good value wine using fruit bought in from all over the state (and make wine for many other vineyards in the region under contract), and Virgin Hills, which is now part of a large wine company called Vincorp, based in Kyneton, few of the Macedon wineries produce more than a couple of thousand cases of wine a year.

All the region needs now is a big company to invest heavily – preferably a French champagne house – and the whole world will know about Macedon.

Macedon flavours

It's difficult to pin down a distinctive regional sparkling wine style in Macedon, because each of the three main producers has such individual house style: Cope-Williams' wines are extremely fine and crisp, Hanging Rock's are big, yeasty and creamy, while Cleveland's wines fit somewhere in the middle. What unites them, perhaps, is the region's ability to produce chardonnay and pinot noir with exceptionally fine, persistent flavour.

Considering how cool it is in the Ranges, the pinot noir produced here by makers such as Bindi and Mount Gisborne can be surprisingly intense and dark, while the best chardonnays from Portree, Bindi and Cobaw Ridge, can have the most scintillating, minerally, pebbly dryness under the crisp, citrussy fruit.

Apart from in a few exceptional sites, the later-ripening cabernet and shiraz often produce quite lean, green wines and as a result some winemakers are moving towards earlier-ripening varieties such as merlot (and in the case of Alan Cooper at Cobaw Ridge, the obscure north Italian variety lagrein) for their fuller-bodied wines. As for other white varieties, riesling can do exceptionally well, gewurztraminer can occasionally produce gently fragrant, steely wines (especially at the almost impossibly small Straws Lane vineyard), and sauvignon blanc is usually right at the very herbaceous, very crisp end of the spectrum.

Bendigo and Heathcote

I've always had a bit of a soft spot for the Bendigo region. This has something to do with the big, cuddly red wines from the vineyards in this warm central Victorian district, but it has more to do with the fact that it's almost exactly as old as I am – or at least the modern incarnation of it is.

In 1968, when I was busy being a mewling and puking infant and making my Mum's life hell, a bloke called Stuart Anderson was busy buying a block of land just outside Bendigo and preparing to plant vines. As I've grown up, so has the region.

There had been vines here before; when the grand city of Bendigo was being built with the profits of the goldfields it supported a thriving local wine industry (then as now, where there are people with disposable cash, you can guarantee the grog sellers are not far behind). There are echoes of this industry reverberating in paddocks and behind trees all over the place: old crumbling ruins that once were wineries, even crude now-empty cellars dug into the red earth, with ghostly chalk inscriptions scrawled onto the rough-hewn roof beams.

The vine louse phylloxera put a crawling end to the Bendigo wine industry in the 1890s, at about the same time that Victoria's economic nosedive put an end to Bendigo city's haughty displays of grandeur. But when the first Balgownie wines started appearing in the 1970s they made jaws drop with their deep fruit and massive structure, and it wasn't long before others were inspired to rush out to Bendigo and stick some vines in the ground.

During the 1980s, at a time when many Australian winemakers were pursuing the cooler cabernet style, Bendigo wineries like Balgownie, Passing Clouds and Chateau Leamon kept the big, ripe shiraz flame burning. And by the end of that decade, vineyards such as Jasper Hill and Mount Ida had established a slightly more elegant variation of that big shiraz style over at Heathcote, in the cooler east of the region.

I have to confess to an even softer spot for Heathcote reds. The

combination of deep red ancient soils and continental climate (hot days, cool nights) is almost perfect for producing intense, powerful but restrained red wines. If I ever lose my marbles completely and decide to plant a vineyard, Heathcote's where I'd go (I'd probably be predictably esoteric, too, and want to plant zinfandel or tempranillo).

But if I do go all the way with this crazy scheme then I certainly won't be alone: the hilly range to the north of the town of Heathcote itself is abuzz with vineyard activity, from small growers playing with a few hectares, to big companies like Brown Brothers bunging in 200 hectares at a time.

The only thing limiting even more explosive growth in Bendigo and Heathcote is water: despite some of the region's most successful vineyards

Lindsay Ross,
winemaker,
Balgownie Estate

(Jasper Hill, Red Edge) being dry-grown, most vignerons feel they need to irrigate to produce a quick, economic and sizeable crop. And water is simply not all that readily available unless you strike it lucky sinking a bore.

Strictly speaking, Bendigo and Heathcote should have separate sections. Right at the end of the 1990s, Heathcote decided to secede from Bendigo, the Heathcote vignerons figuring that their climate and their wines were different enough, and there was enough development to justify going it alone. All seemed to be running smoothly until, in grand modern Australian wine industry fashion, disagreement bubbled up over the proposed boundaries of the new Heathcote GI – disagreements that, at the time of writing, haven't been resolved. So, for now at least, Heathcote remains an appendage.

Bendigo and Heathcote flavours

Despite the fact that some very lovely whites can be produced here (Jasper Hill's fragrant riesling, Water Wheel's full-flavoured chardonnay and The Heathcote Winery's intriguing, minerally viognier spring readily to mind), this is very much red wine country.

Shiraz is undoubtedly king. It produces rich, round, mouth-filling wines in Bendigo, often with a streak of what one old taster evocatively described as sandalwood, and often complemented by the sweet vanilla and coconut of new American oak – best producers are Balgownie, Passing Clouds, Water Wheel, Chateau Leamon and Blackjack. In Heathcote, the wines are slightly less round but can be even more intense, tightly coiled, with a streak of dried herbs rather than sandalwood – best producers are Jasper Hill, Wild Duck Creek (beware the ultra-powerful Duck Muck) and Red Edge.

If shiraz is king, though, cabernet sauvignon is the crown prince: at Balgownie and Red Edge it can produce immense, dense, tannic wines that flood the mouth with flavour. And if we push the analogy even further, then merlot and malbec are the palace guards, waiting to overthrow the royal family in a bloody coup: recent wines made from these two varieties, particularly from the new Munari vineyard at Heathcote, are encouragingly plush and ripe, the malbec particularly shimmering with pepper and spice.

Goulburn Valley

The Goulburn Valley is a wine writer's dream. Yes, the wines are good, and yes, the scenery's romantic and thoroughly Australian, but that's not what makes it a dream. It's the big, fat, heavy symbolism of the place that turns me on.

Right in the middle of the region, staring at each other across the Goulburn River, sit two wineries. One, Chateau Tahbilk, was founded in 1860 and absolutely reeks of Victoria's nineteenth-century wine history. Its archly weird pagoda-like tower and magnificent old underground cellars heave with tradition. Its old established garden and roses and the gently babbling waters of the Goulburn River create an immensely calm atmosphere. The red wines that third generation winemaker Alister Purbrick produces are as consciously old-fashioned as their labels – savoury, tannic, aged in old oak, from another era. And the block of shiraz vines planted in 1860 that miraculously escaped phylloxera are like a holy grail to the shiraz-loving pilgrim.

The other winery, Mitchelton, was established almost exactly a century after Tahbilk, in the late 1960s, and is just as strong a symbol, this time of the modern Victorian wine industry. There's a tower here, too, a weird-looking pointy diamond-shaped viewing platform on top of a big stalk. The bright, clean lines of the cellar door and restaurant buildings have held up pretty well against changing tastes in architecture. The wines produced by Don Lewis, Mitchelton's winemaker since the beginning, are thoroughly modern: ripe, clean, often wrapped in sophisticated new oak. And the vineyard is constantly changing, with experiments involving yield and irrigation always being trialed.

Considering how well these two vineyards make wine, and considering the wonderful histories they have crammed behind their walls and in their vats, it's surprising there aren't more wineries in the Goulburn Valley. Although there are many growers with fairly large blocks of land, making full use of the reliable warm climate, there are only a dozen or so other wineries in the region – with David Traeger and Monichino arguably the best of them.

Actually, to be perfectly accurate, I should be referring to the regions, plural, because the wineries grouped around Nagambie in the south of the region (Tahbilk, Mitchelton, Traeger, etc.), have recently broken away from the Goulburn Valley and announced they were now the region of Nagambie Lakes (the idea being to promote the notion of a slightly cooler climate that proximity to water creates).

Again, it was only a matter of time. Just as there has always been a

Don Lewis,
winemaker,
Mitchelton

clear flavour difference between Heathcote and the rest of Bendigo, so there is a clear difference between the wines in the south of the Goulburn Valley (called the Upper Goulburn) and those in the much warmer north of the region, towards the Murray River (confusingly called the Lower Goulburn). Perplexed? Boggled? I am a little, which is why I've chickened out and stuck to the easy-to-conceptualise, catch-all Goulburn Valley tag.

Goulburn Valley flavours

A lot of people – the French, in particular – believe that the best wines taste of where they're from, as well as what they're made from and how they were made. If you ever had any doubts at all about whether this might be true, drive through the Goulburn Valley in summer, then taste a Goulburn Valley cabernet. The great silent massiveness of the bush, its long dirt roads and ancient white gums – all this seems to be there in the wine in your mouth, But also, running through it like the river running through the dry country, you'll taste a core of ripe sweet fruit (sometimes I surprise myself with what a romantic bugger I can be).

Again, white wines valiantly soldier on here, and, in the form of marsanne, have even developed a regional speciality (crisp and unwooded at Tahbilk, oak-aged and richer at Mitchelton). Riesling can be surprisingly good (surprising given the warm climate), as can other white varieties such as chardonnay and viognier (both in a fatter, riper style).

But again, the red wines are the heroes: big, old-fashioned, fantastically rustic cabernet and shiraz at Tahbilk and David Traeger; more polished, sweeter, new-oaky versions of both varieties at Mitchelton, the shiraz usually a lot gutsier than the cabernet. As for other red varieties, they are in the minority: there's some malbec at Tahbilk, merlot at Mitchelton and patches of old grenache and mourvedre snuck away in corners of the region, all of which do very well in the climate, but the land here ultimately belongs to shiraz and cabernet.

The High Country

Sometimes Australian wineries can be really annoying. Because there's so much bloody freedom in this country – the freedom to plant whatever grape varieties you want, wherever you want – vineyards and wineries are always popping up just outside the boundaries of accepted regions. This is fine and dandy for the wineries and the consumer, who couldn't give a damn where the wine's from as long as it tastes good, but it's a pain in the bum for people like me who have to pigeonhole everybody to make them fit nicely in a book.

That's what used to happen with the Central Victorian High Country. Just to the south east of the Goulburn Valley, the land rises into the Strathbogie Ranges, and continues building east past Mansfield into the lower parts of the Victorian snowfields. Within this broad, high area are a collection of quite disparate vineyards and wineries, from Murrindindi in the south to Mount Helen in the north, and from Plunketts in the west to Delatite in the east.

A few years ago, these seemingly disparate wineries were shovelled into the Victorian High Country sack for convenience's sake. Then more and more people began planting vineyards (Domaine Chandon in the Yarra Valley, for example, have large plantings up here for their sparkling wine) and it began to look and feel like a real region. On top of that, people started noticing that there were more similarities than differences between the wine styles of Plunkett, Delatite, Murrindindi and so on. So the lot of them decided it was time to do this regional identity thing properly.

What defines this large region is the coolness and the altitude: Ros Ritchie at Delatite and Sam Plunkett at Plunketts both proudly show you photographs of their vineyards either covered in snow or looking across to snow-covered mountains. And, as we've seen, what coolness and altitude bring to a wine is finesse and intensity of fruit flavour.

High Country flavours

Although much of the fruit grown in the High Country is used for sparkling wine, very little makes its way into High Country-labelled fizz (the exception being a bubbly from Delatite). You're much more likely to come across table wines up here. At the crisp, aromatic end, there is really fine, tight green-appley riesling and fragrant gewurz (evocatively named Dead Man's Hill) produced by Delatite, and a fine semillon sauvignon produced by Plunkett. Chardonnay is, as you'd expect, in the cool-climate mould here, with Murrindindi chardonnay full of mouth-watering grapefruit and toast flavours when it's young.

Some lighter-bodied, spicy, peppery shiraz has been produced here, as has pretty good pinot noir. The most distinctive style of High Country red, though, is made from cabernet and/or merlot, with a clear peppermint edge to the aromas and flavours in the case of Delatite and more of a leafy, cedary, herbal character in the wines from Mount Helen.

We're coming in to land at a small airstrip near Mount Beauty, in the Alpine country in north-east Victoria. The small, six-seater I'm in has bounced over Mount Buller and Mount Buffalo and is now banking at an impossible angle to swing round for landing. Then I see that there are cows on the strip. Um, excuse me Mr Pilot, but I think there are cows on the, um strip? The plane buzzes them a couple of times (down, round, up, round, *eeeurgh*) and finally we make it down onto the soft grass, where I get out, legs trembling, stomach churning, and take a lung full of the crisp morning mountain air.

This is sensational country up here, best appreciated, I am prepared to grudgingly admit, from the air. The deeply folded mountains and valleys of the Great Dividing Range roll all the way up the eastern seaboard into northern New South Wales, and on a clear-dawn morning at 20,000 feet you feel you can see all the way to the end. Dramatic as the country is, though, its picturesque qualities are not what I'm really concerned with here. I'm much more interested in how its high peaks and low dips provide an enormous diversity of sites for growing grapes – from the warm flats around Milawa, up through the cooler valleys of the King, Ovens and Kiewa Rivers, and finally up to the high country vineyards at Beechworth and Whitlands.

This part of the world has been known for its wines since the days of the gold rush, when places like Beechworth and Wangaratta were major regional centres, swarming with suddenly rich prospectors and the inevitable gaggle of grocers and grog floggers that were always one step behind them. While most of the vineyards disappeared when the gold ran out and phylloxera ran in, one family, the Brown brothers of Milawa, managed to hold on to its vineyards, partly by maintaining a steady business with the Italian community who had settled in the area and planted tobacco.

For most of the twentieth century Brown Brothers had the region pretty much to themselves, pioneering varietal table wines and wine styles

at a time when most of the industry was concerned with bulk sales and fortifieds. Then, in the 1970s and 80s, when the wine boom boomed, some King Valley farmers began to turn paddocks into vineyards, and the region's now-thriving grape industry took off, with many of the struggling Italian tobacco farmers bitten by the grape growing bug. I say grape industry because the vineyards far outweigh the number of wineries in the region. Most of the fruit picked off the thousands of hectares of vines here is sold for use in wines made outside its boundaries, with large companies such as De Bortoli, Kingston Estate and Miranda establishing huge processing facilities in the King Valley just to make wine for use in their cheaper brands. That's not to say there isn't an exciting future for small wineries in the north-east. Apart from Brown Brothers, who go from strength to strength (and couldn't be called a small winery), a number of small producers such as Wood Park, Pizzini and Chrismont in the King Valley, Boynton's of Bright in the Ovens Valley and Giaconda and Sorrenberg up at Beechworth are all making good – sometimes absolutely stunning – wines from their own vineyards.

The north-east's main attraction, though, can also be its undoing. You see, in most of the region, particularly in the warmer parts of the King Valley, the combination of fertile soils and generally good rainfall can result in high crops and very vigorous vines. For the big companies, this is a major plus, because most years the King Valley receives enough sun to ripen those high crops and produce lots of good-flavoured wine relatively cheaply. For the smaller, more quality-conscious producer, though, keeping yields down to concentrate flavour and ensure ripening means that grape growing here can be much more demanding. Yields are not so much of a problem in the coolest parts of the north-east or in the drier, leaner soils of Beechworth, and it's from here that the better wines often come.

Name your poison. Because of its diversity of climate and soil, the north-east can and does produce absolutely everything from fine, crisp sparkling to luscious muscat (another reason why big companies like to have access to vineyards here: it's the viticultural equivalent of a supermarket – a few thousand litres of chardonnay, some cabernet on special, oh and a couple of tankerloads of merlot, please).

Some varieties and styles stand out, though. Riesling and sauvignon blanc from the higher, cooler parts of the King Valley can have very lively, aromatic intensity (and the riesling can age well, as Brown Brothers have proved). Likewise, the Brown Brothers sparkling wines from their very high and cold Whitlands vineyard are excellent, and a lot of fruit from the region is used by the big companies in their sparkling wine blends. Chardonnay absolutely excels at Beechworth in an almost impossibly intense, finely structured style, the quality-obsessed Rick Kinzbrunner of Giaconda managing to position his chardonnay as one of the country's top half-dozen (with Barry Morey's Sorrenberg chardonnay not far behind).

Cabernet and shiraz do well, particularly in the better, north-facing spots, producing tight, grainy, medium bodied wines. I am more excited by the potential of merlot, though, if the highly gluggable, approachable, currant-and-spice flavoured, excellent-value wines I've tasted so far are anything to go by – it may not produce an earth-shattering wine up here, but it can make a good, solid, reliable drink.

Not surprisingly, given the region's strong Italian heritage (the annual festival at Myrtleford in the Ovens Valley is a showcase of salami-making and traditional Italian cooking), many growers are also experimenting with sangiovese, nebbiolo and barbera, among other Italian grapes. Again, like merlot, early wines produced from these varieties are very exciting – which kind of makes sense, because in parts the King Valley in particular has more than a touch of northern Italy about it – the deep-sided valleys, the pine trees, the gentle babbling streams. If the Italian varietal thing ever becomes a full-blown trend, the King Valley is well placed to supply.

Rutherglen and Glenrowan

God bless Rutherglen. I'm not a religious man, nor am I a particularly fervent patriot, but I'd be happy to see this region in northeast Victoria either sainted or given an Order of Australia for its services to wine. Despite phylloxera infestations, despite dramatic changes in public taste, despite two world wars and despite countless recessions, Rutherglen has soldiered on, pumping out heroic reds and extraordinary fortifieds from its scraggly vineyards and old wineries. It deserves some kind of medal – but our undying gratitude, unquestioning love and continued support might have to do.

To understand how Rutherglen survived the twentieth century when almost every other wine region in Victoria disappeared, you have to hurl yourself back to the 1860s, when this country was crawling with gold diggers and merchants and hangers-on and young families, all out to find their fortunes in the New World.

It must have been a dusty, hot, hard life for these new settlers – especially the Campbells, Morrises, Smiths and Chambers, Scottish and English families who may have been prepared for Rutherglen's wickedly cold winter's nights but would have been beaten around by its hard summer days. The hardship didn't stop them dreaming or taking opportunities, though, and by the height of its boom, these families and others had made Rutherglen home to vast areas of vineyard – some, like All Saints, with extraordinary, grand, castle-like wineries attached.

Initially, these vineyards provided a sea of wine for the miners and did a booming trade with Melbourne, but when the Victorian economy went belly up in the 1890s and phylloxera struck the vineyards, things looked like collapsing. Luckily, Rutherglen had established a strong export market to London for its big reds – and a few decades later for its fortifieds – so the vignerons could afford to replant their decimated vineyards on phylloxera-resistant rootstocks. This kept the region alive, with extra sales to the newly arrived Italian migrants in the 1950s helping things along.

Then in the 1960s, Rutherglen began what has now become a

state-wide (country-wide) phenomenon: the annual wine festival. This really put the region on the map for a whole new generation, and ensured it would live to see another century (at least): the trek up to Rutherglen for an audience with one of the living winemaking legends became a popular weekend ritual for many Melburnians, most of whom came back with a big drum of big red that they'd then bottle at home and reverentially sip on as if it was mother's milk.

left: Malcolm (left) and
Colin Campbell, viticulturist
and winemaker, Campbells

right: David Morris,
winemaker, Morris Wines

Glenrowan, on the other side of the Warby Ranges to the south, is slightly cooler than Rutherglen, but still produces some big red wines and luscious fortifieds. Baileys, established in 1870, and Booth's Taminick, first planted a quarter-century later, have both managed to survive into the modern world using their reputations for blackstrap, monumental shiraz wines as a life raft. Baileys makes good muscat and tokay, too, but it's the famous shiraz in the red-stripe label, made from vines planted in the first decades of the twentieth century that most people think of when the Bailey name is intoned.

Rutherglen and Glenrowan flavours

Oh, look, I'm not even going to bother talking about the white varieties in Rutherglen and Glenrowan: there are some white wines made (surprisingly good riesling, even), but they're few and far between and they pale in comparison with the reds and the stickies. So let's just get stuck into them, shall we?

Over the last few years the Rutherglen winemakers have been busy trying to convince the world that they're not just fortified producers. We listened politely, and tried their red wines, and had to admit they had a point. We loved the rather lovely, intensely dark Bobbie Burns shiraz from Campbells, we revelled in the hugely earthy, take-no-prisoners red blends from Bullers, we staggered a little after trying the monumental durif (a regional speciality) from Stanton and Killeen, and we even rather enjoyed the rich and deep sparkling red from All Saints.

We also admitted that the region was experiencing a mini-revolution in red winemaking style, with relative newcomers such as Andrew Sutherland Smith at Warrabilla and Max Cofield at Cofield (the first from an old Rutherglen family, the second an experienced Rutherglen winemaker) fashioning wines with all the power and oomph we'd come to expect from this part of the world, but with a little more refinement and polish.

But then we cracked and asked if it wouldn't be too much trouble for the winemakers to let us have a taste of their absolutely sensational, mind-blowingly luscious muscats and tokays. I mean, we couldn't go on being polite forever.

No, hold on, where am I? I'm standing in a vineyard staring at a panoramic backdrop of dusky gum forests, parched paddocks and the tumble-down blue of the Great

Dividing Range. It all looks very Australian: there's even a bloke in a Drizabone running up and down the vine rows in a battered old Holden ute. But the winemaker and viticulturist I'm with are talking in French about the pétanque tournament scheduled for the weekend in town. What the hell's going on?

The French influence is a strong one in Victoria's Pyrenees. The region's first vineyard and winery of the modern era (yes, there was a wine industry here, too, in the nineteenth century) was planted in the early 1960s by the huge French company Rémy Martin, initially for brandy production, but more recently for sparkling and table wines. And the third winery to be established here, Taltarni in 1972, although owned by a Californian, has had for most of its existence a French-born winemaker/manager, Dominique Portet (Portet has now left, but the French accent survives in the shape of Taltarni's vineyard manager, Phillippe Bru).

Portet and another Bordeaux-born Frenchman, Vincent Gere, until recently the Blue Pyrenees chief winemaker, wrought their wines in thoroughly Gallic fashion – Taltarni's cabernet was, in the early years, as tannic and brusque as a young Bordeaux, while Gere and now his successor, Kim Hart, have applied meticulous care to the Blue Pyrenees sparkling wines and turned them into surprisingly delicate fizz, considering that the region's warmth is much more inclined to produce big, heavy flavours.

The Pyrenees is unique in that these two main establishing wineries were, from the very start, designed to be substantial operations. No piss-farting around with a couple of boutique producers encouraging others to join them and slowly building up a reputation: in the Pyrenees it happened the other way round. Chateau Remy (now known as Blue Pyrenees Estate) and Taltarni arrived with a bang in the 1970s, and were then followed by a clutch of smaller wineries, some of which turned into larger ones with time.

It's with these other wineries that the French theme begins to dissolve

and disappear completely. At Warrenmang, Italian-born Luigi Bazzani runs a magnificent country restaurant and turns out some big, brawny red wines. At Dalwhinnie, across the road from Taltarni, David Jones produces some stunningly spicy, intense shiraz, and powerful quince-like chardonnay, both with elements of European style to them but ultimately very much in the central Victorian mode. And at Summerfield, we kiss any vestige of European finesse goodbye: Ian and Mark Summerfield's rich,

left: Kim Hart, winemaker,
Blue Pyrenees Estate

right: David Jones,
winemaker, Dalwhinnie

powerful and extremely ripe shirazes are unashamedly big Aussie wines.

The Pyrenees region is a fairly broad one, stretching from very warm country up near St Arnaud down to some cooler spots around Avoca and the boldly named Amphitheatre. This can result in some sub-regional differences: the cabernets produced by Neil Robb at Redbank in the warm north are much sturdier, much more tannic than those produced by Matt Barry at Mount Avoca in the cooler south, for example.

Until recently, this wide area was home to only nine wineries, almost all of which had been established before 1980. Then, in the late 1990s, a flurry of plantings and building saw three new wineries – Peerick, Amherst and Berry's Bridge – and big new vineyards like Southcorp's 150 hectares at Elmhurst burst onto the scene. It looks as though the Pyrenees is gearing up for a very exciting twenty-first century.

Pyrenees flavours

The idea that within one region you can make both a delicate sparkling and a full-on, blockbuster shiraz is a typically Australian one. European vignerons tend to concentrate on one or two styles in each region, and do those two styles well. Here, because there's nothing stopping winemakers making any style they want, that's precisely what many of them do – make anything and everything.

Having said that, though, people are realising that the Pyrenees is essentially big red country. Some very good chardonnays have come out of the region (Dalwhinnie, Blue Pyrenees) and it can produce excellent sauvignon blanc and even viognier (both at Taltarni), but the best wines of all are made from cabernet and shiraz, either on their own (Taltarni, Summerfield, Berry's Bridge, Dalwhinnie) or blended together (Blue Pyrenees, Redbank 'Sally's Paddock').

Whether it's the shiraz or the cabernet, though, there is very often an underlying mintiness to the red wines here, combined with sturdy, sometimes really powerful tannins. This makes Pyrenees reds good keepers, developing great complexity and mellowing over the years into great wines for drinking with game and mushrooms in the warm country-style restaurant at Warrenmang.

The Grampians

So it's the 1860s and you're a gold prospector, been out from England working the fields near Ballarat in western Victoria for ten years now, except that the gold's begun to dry up and you don't quite know what to do with yourself . Until, that is, you're drinking in a wine saloon in Stawell one day and one of the locals, a young French feller who helps his sister run a vineyard up the road, says that a bloke called Joseph Best is looking for workers to help him dig out some cellars beneath his winery for storing wine in. So you rock up to the winery, called Great Western, and Best gives you a job. You spend the next few months shovelling and pickaxing your way through the soft chalky soil. Little do you know that, well over a century later, the tunnels you have helped to dig will have become one of the Australian wine industry's most magical spaces.

I've spent a fair bit of time down in those 'drives' at Great Western. They're now owned by Seppelt, who bought the place in 1918 from a guy called Hans Irvine, who had established a major business for sparkling wine matured in the drives. It's a spooky atmosphere down there: it's acoustically dead, so when you speak, you feel as though the walls soak your voice up like a sponge. The tunnels are covered in a soft black mould, like roughly torn felt, a naturally occurring growth that contributes a gentle nuttiness and humidity to the air you breathe. But most importantly, the temperature is a constant cool, regardless of what it's like on the surface. I've been at Great Western on a 35-degree summer's afternoon and in the frosty grip of a minus-7-degree winter morning, and the temperature in the drives has always been the same.

The drives aren't the only magical place at Great Western. Just up the road is Best's, established in 1866 by Joseph's brother, Henry. There is a magnificent old cellar here, too, still used, and a block of ancient vines planted in 1867 – including pinot meunier, which the current owner/winemaker, Viv Thomson, makes into an earthy, grainy wine that can't taste too dissimilar to the nineteenth-century wines of Great Western.

Much of the region's huge personality stems from the fact that it's been producing wine continuously since it was founded; you feel like the culture of the vine has permeated Great Western's big red gums and filled its broad, low valleys, clinging to the old vine rows hugging the contours of the hill. You wander across the road from the huge sparkling winemaking facility that Seppelt has now become and through the old cemetery, and you're surrounded by ghosts: most of the region's pioneers are buried here.

What Great Western became known for more than anything was sparkling wine, thanks to Irvine and Seppelt, a reputation reinforced by the fact that most of the fizz in the Southcorp group, from Seppelt Salinger down to Killawarra brut, is made here. But Great Western, or the Grampians as it is now called (referring to the massive mountain country to the west), is not actually a great place to grow pinot noir or chardonnay, the modern fizzmaker's favourite grapes. It is, rather, a special place for shiraz – warm enough to get good, ripe flavours, but cool enough to give the resulting wines a distinctive spicy, peppery edge and the ability to age superbly.

As well as the old wineries and vineyards around Great Western itself, the Grampians region includes a number of other, more recent arrivals. A little further back towards Ararat, for example, some ex-Seppelt winemakers are making hugely regional wines from old established shiraz vineyards – Warren Randall and Brian Fletcher at Garden Gully (quite an achievement considering the two are based in McLaren Vale and Margaret River, respectively), and Tony Royal at Armstrong vineyard. And past Ararat, off the Western Highway towards Melbourne, Trevor Mast's Mount Langi Ghiran vineyard regularly produces some of the finest shiraz in the country, very much in a leaner, more concentrated, peppery style.

Grampians flavours

Riesling can do well here, producing really floral, perfumed, citrussy wines that can age well. Langi Ghiran also produce a ripe, melony pinot grigio. Cabernet sauvignon can be excellent, especially blended with merlot in a fine, poised, intensely berryish style. There are even old plantings of traditional varieties, tenaciously squeezing out tiny quantities of old-fashioned wines: the broad white chasselas and ondenc, for example, and the quirky old dolcetto (thought to be malbec for years) and pinot meunier at Best's.

But the best variety in the Grampians is shiraz (you could feel that 'but' coming, couldn't you?), whether it's producing the rich black wines of Garden Gully and Armstrong; the focussed, peppery wines of Langi Ghiran; or the very fine, elegant, ripe but reserved wines made from the oldest vineyards at Seppelt or Best's (particularly Best's stunning 'Thomson Family' reserve bottling). Colin Preece, Seppelt's winemaker for thirty years in the middle of the twentieth century, had a knack for coaxing the best out of his shiraz vineyards: the legendary wines he made in the 1950s were based around it and still taste alarmingly ripe, young and full of liquoricey life fifty years later.

Ripe Great Western shiraz from very old vines is also the secret to the success of Seppelt's Show Sparkling Shiraz, arguably the model for the style in Australia. A glass of Seppelt Show and a plate of kangaroo at the Kookaburra restaurant in Hall's Gap, right up in the Grampian mountains themselves, and you really feel you're doing the regional gastronomy thing properly.

Trevor Mast,
winemaker,
Mount Langi Ghiran

The far south-west of Victoria, with its vast open grazing land, its long, low dry stone walls, and its century-old houses with their characteristic whitewashed walls and green roofs, is in many ways the last place you'd expect to find vineyards. It's really cold down here and there is little passing trade other than the odd adventurous soul who veers off the Great Ocean Road twisting its way from Melbourne to Adelaide.

And yet there they are. Vineyards. And more of them are appearing all the time.

It was a Seppelt – Karl – who decided in 1964 that Drumborg, a windswept spot north of Portland, right on the coast, would be a good place for white grapes. Ten years later, the Crawford River vineyard was established by local farmer John Thomson and soon a couple of others such as Kingsley, in Portland, had joined them.

These early grape growers had a pretty tough time of it, but they persisted and were eventually rewarded with some excellent wines. Riesling from Crawford River and Drumborg can be simply stunning, with really tight, piercing limey aroma and a crisp, endless palate. John Thomson also makes a very good semillon sauvignon, and Seppelt have made some encouraging early wines from pinot gris. Crawford River manages to get cabernet and merlot ripe enough in most years to produce a really attractive, extremely elegant red, while Drumborg cabernet seldom loses its hard green edge. What the Drumborg vineyard has done well – and consistently – is produce some great chardonnay and pinot noir for sparkling wines. Most of it goes into blends, but some of this wines has seen the cold light of day as one-off bottlings, and has been very fine indeed.

Back towards Melbourne, sparkling wine is also a style many would associate with Ballarat. Because it's here, just outside the city at Smythsdale, that Ian Home established the Yellowglen winery in 1975. Yellowglen, of course, is now one of Australia's most successful sparkling wine brands, and for many years, the winery Home built and Mildara Blass bought was the only one in the region, processing fruit trucked in from all over the country. In the last few decade or so, though, a host of small vineyards and wineries has appeared on the Ballarat scene, dribbling tiny quantities of sometimes really good wines into the trade.

This is uncompromisingly cool-climate wine country: Ballarat is high on a wet plateau and, I swear, is always shrouded in drizzle every time I drive to it or through it. Rod Stott's lean and zippy sauvignon blanc from the Dulcinea Vineyard and Norm Latta's lovely pinot noir from the Eastern Peake vineyard are encouraging signs that, with a few more impassioned souls mad enough to plant here, the Ballarat region could have an exciting future.

To the north-east of Ballarat, heading towards the Macedon Ranges, there are also some vineyards dotted around the spa towns of Daylesford and Hepburn Springs. There used to be a thriving Italian community here in the nineteenth century, and at least one of the new vineyards, Colin and Rosa Mitchell's tiny Yandoit Hills, is reviving this tradition by growing and making nebbiolo.

Rod Stott's lean and zippy sauvignon blanc from the Dulcinea Vineyard and Norm Latta's lovely pinot noir from the Eastern Peake vineyard are encouraging signs that, with a few more impassioned souls mad enough to plant here, the Ballarat region could have an exciting future.

Gippsland

The idea that you can lump under one regional heading a group of wineries and vineyards as widely scattered as those in south-east Victoria is kind of ridiculous, surely? Well maybe it is, but that's what's happened in Gippsland.

Gippsland's easternmost winery, Wyanga Park, is roughly 200 kilometres as the cockatoo flies from its westernmost winery, Phillip Island Wines. And the region's southernmost winery, the cool and wet Windy Ridge, down near Wilson's Promontory, is buffeted by climatic influences quite different to those affecting wineries such as the warmer, drier Nicholson River, 160 kilometres further north-east.

So to make things a little easier to grasp, the Gippsland growers have loosely grouped themselves under sub-regional headings. Most wineries are in South Gippsland, confusingly in the west of the region, down around Leongatha. A few, the West Gippsland wineries, are located in the centre of the region, in the La Trobe Valley around Morwell, while the rest – the East Gippsland wineries – actually are right over in the east towards the New South Wales border. I suspect, though, that as more vineyards are planted and wineries established, it's only a matter of time before these sub-regions become more clearly defined, with more distinct identities perhaps behind new, more appropriate names.

In 1886, the Yarra Valley vineyard owner Hubert de Castella wrote a book called *John Bull's Vineyard*. In it he described a rail journey to Sale, in east Gippsland, through the magnificent forests that then made up much of the countryside. He was full of hope for this part of Victoria, particularly for the future of the vine, despite the fact that nobody at the time shared his viticultural vision.

As happened in most of the rest of the state, a few pioneer nineteenth-century vignerons did plant vineyards and make wine in Gippsland, but they didn't last long into the twentieth century: the dairy and logging industries took over and still have a hold on the area (Gippsland is renowned for the richness of its cream and cheese). It wasn't until the boutique boom of the 1970s and 80s that Gippsland was explored once more by people with a twinkle in their eye and the taste of wine in their mouths.

Although a couple of the region's best wineries have produced some stunning wines over the last few decades, and although the large companies have taken fruit out to use in blends – even contracting large vineyards specifically for this purpose – Gippsland remains staunchly boutique in focus. There are about twenty wineries, most family owned and run, and most producing no more than 1000 cases a year – many much fewer.

It's those few stunning wines, though, that have given Gippsland its enviable reputation – the peerless pinot noirs of Bass Phillip, the hedonistic chardonnays of Nicholson River, and, more recently, the very stylish, refined wines from the permanently-netted vineyards on Phillip Island (there more for protection from the wind than the birds). Again, it's only a matter of time, I suspect, before some major investments are made and we see Gippsland wine become wider known.

Gippsland flavours

Pinot noir and chardonnay are way out in front as the most successful wine styles in Gippsland. At its South Gippsland best, from low-yielding vineyards and meticulous winemakers like Phillip Jones at Bass Phillip, pinot noir can be sensationally complex, dense and lingering, its dark cherry and plum fruit developing really sexy, mushroomy, soy sauce characters with age. Chardonnay varies much more in style, from the crisp, oatmealy flavours from cooler vineyards like Paradise Enough in South Gippsland, to the richly textured, buttery, golden chardonnays from warmer vineyards such as Narkoojee, Briagolong and Nicholson River further north and east.

Other red grapes such as shiraz, merlot and cabernet are grown here, but tend towards the greener, lighter styles in anything but warm vintages. Having said that, of the three, merlot will probably end up being the most popular, if the very good, occasional varietal bottlings from the McAlister vineyard are any indication. Of the other whites grown, my favourite is sauvignon blanc (not that many Gippsland vineyards other than Phillip Island have it planted): the cool climate produces wines with the kind of brisk zing that I like.

The Tyranny of Distance

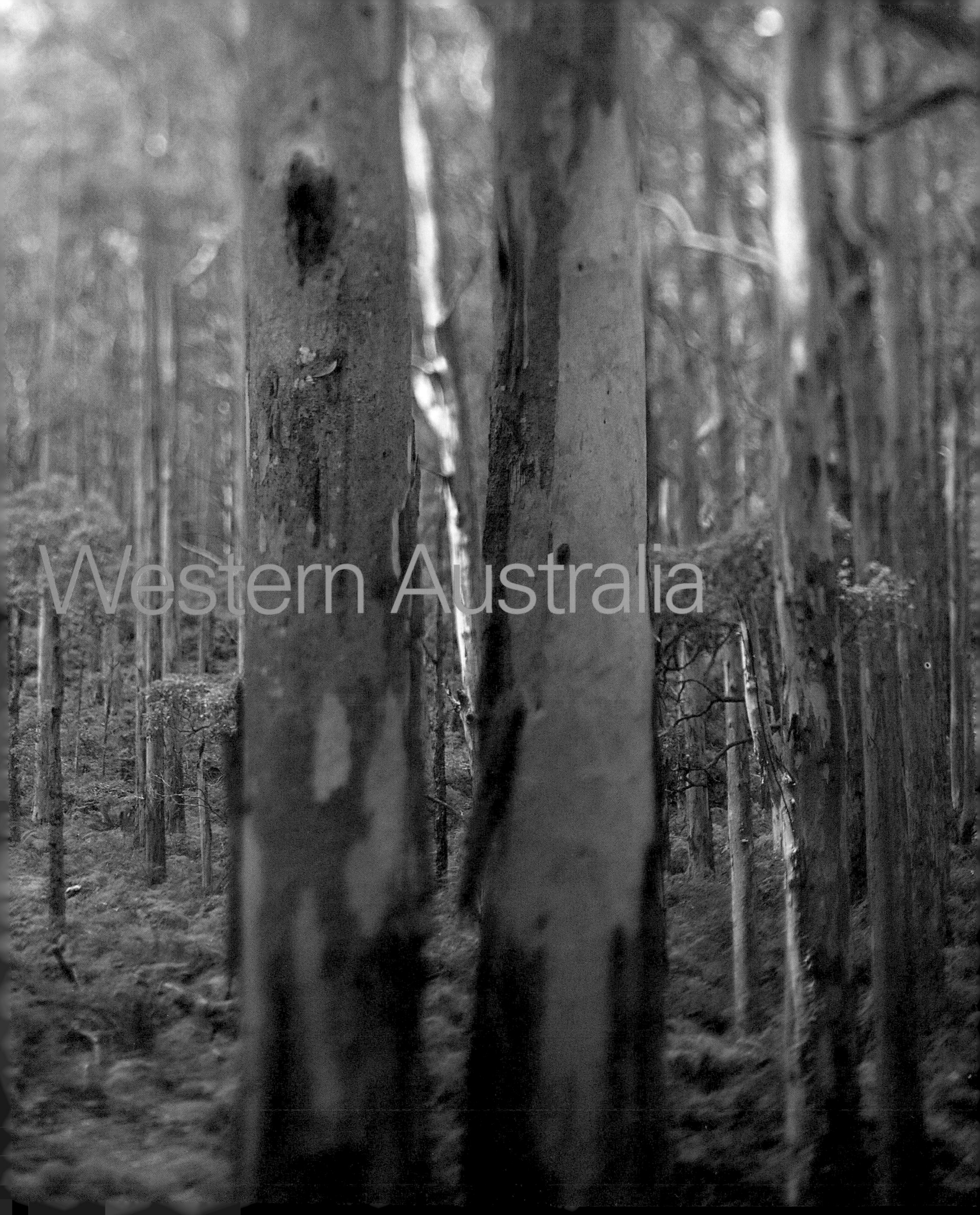
Western Australia

West Australian Wine Regions

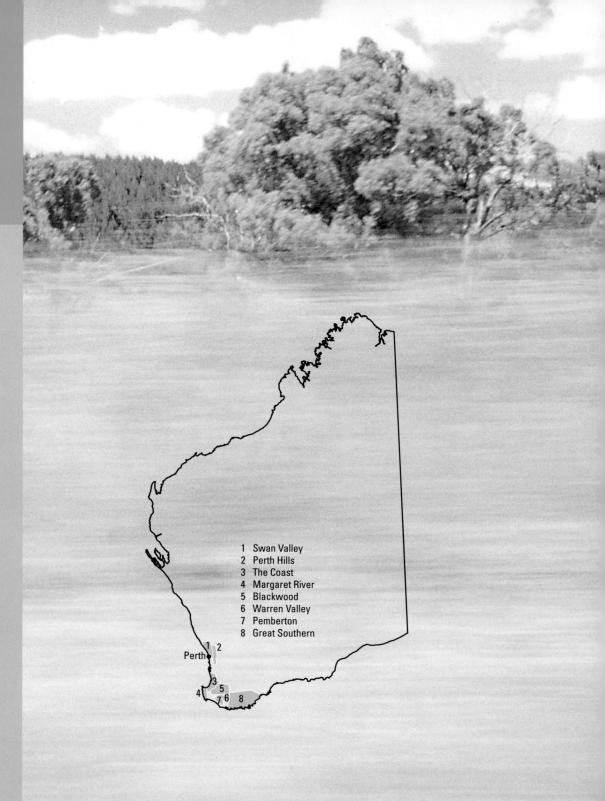

1 Swan Valley
2 Perth Hills
3 The Coast
4 Margaret River
5 Blackwood
6 Warren Valley
7 Pemberton
8 Great Southern

Perth

It's a four hour flight from the west coast to the east. Sounds the first line of like a song, doesn't it, but if you've ever done the soul-sapping red-eye trip from Perth, when the time difference robs you of a full night's sleep, you'll know that the last thing you want to do when you get off that plane is sing.

The point I'm trying to make is that the wine regions of Western Australia are a bloody long way from those concentrated around the south-eastern tip of the country. More importantly, they're four hours by plane – or a few days by truck – from the wine shops and restaurants of Melbourne, Sydney and Brisbane. You might as well be selling to another country – indeed, WA historically has always done well in export markets, because anywhere outside Perth virtually *is* an export market.

So it's remote. And it's small: the WA industry as a whole only produces about two per cent of Australia's wine. But the vast majority of that two per cent is premium: what WA lacks in volume, it more than makes up for in quality. The amount of good press that the best wines of WA receive is also out of all proportion to their size.

Wine has been made in Western Australia since the early 1800s, but the last thirty years have seen the place really take off. As people have left the warm and comfortable regions around Perth and boldly gone down south and up into the hills, they have discovered whole new worlds of flavour and new wine styles that have rewritten the rule books for Australian wine. I reckon Margaret River or Pemberton would be possibly the best places in the country to plant a vineyard – if only they weren't so far away.

The Coast

You're driving, driving, driving down the Old Coast Road south of Perth, and suddenly you pass a sign pointing to a winery. Further down – much further down – past Bunbury, on your way to Margaret River, more signs appear and then, just as quickly, they're gone.

Until recently, the few vineyards and wineries that stretched from Perth to Busselton at the northern boundary of Margaret River were lumped under the heading South West Coastal Plain, which kind of gave you an idea of where they were but no idea of how different they could be. Now, there is a clear distinction between those in the north, around Mandurah, and those in the Geographe region down south, around Capel and Donnybrook.

The vineyards near Mandurah, notably Peel Estate and Baldivis Estate, enjoy a climate slightly cooler than those regions north of Perth and, being closer to the sea, benefit more from the sea breezes. They are still very warm, though, and can produce wines with robust flavours (and in some cases at Peel Estate, hefty alcohol). Peel Estate in particular is notable for its incredible Tuart sand soils: the vines look as though they've been planted in some flat forgotten white sand dune, but somehow, like the tall gums that surround them, they manage to thrive.

Those Tuart sands crop up again at Capel, where wineries such as Capel Vale and Killerby have established a solid reputation for the region over the last twenty years – in Killerby's case by concentrating on estate-grown wines, and in Capel Vale's case by also sourcing fruit from outside Geographe. Again, it's still warm country down here – especially inland, at Donnybrook, where the soil is richer – but just that little bit cooler than Mandurah, producing wines with a little more finesse. Some of the largest recent vineyard developments have been in the Fergusson Valley, north of Donnybrook, while there are enough vineyards now even further inland in the Blackwood Valley for that region to have established its own regional identity. This is definitely a part of WA worth watching.

Coastal flavours

Will Nairn at Peel Estate has been making some of WA's most robust wines for years: his shiraz and zinfandel in particular can be absolutely loaded with pruney, dark earthy fruit flavours, with the zin regularly packing a big wallop of alcohol. Nairn can also do well with chenin blanc and verdelho, making off-dry, pleasant wines.

At Geographe, the robustness is toned down a little, and some good, full-flavoured chardonnays start appearing, as well as crisper, more fragrant verdelho and semillon–sauvignon blanc blends. The reds lighten up a little down here, with good, cedary, grainy tannin cabernet–merlot blends and some vibrant, spicy mid-weight shiraz coming from Capel Vale.

Margaret River

I have a theory about Margaret River. I suspect that the reason its wines keep getting so much sensational press from the world's wine media has nothing to do with the fact that the wines can be excellent and everything to do with the fact that Margaret River itself is absolute heaven on earth. You can write *nice* things about the place from tasting the wines – but if you go there and spend time there, you just can't help writing the most *extravagantly gushing* things about the place.

No, seriously, there really is something special about Margaret River. The magnificent karri forests in the region's national parks; the often staggeringly beautiful vineyard sites; the saturated, glowing light of a perfect summer's day; the ever-present rumble of the Indian Ocean; the soft sea breezes which cut the heat – it's all too good to be true (see what I mean?).

You've got to love a wine region, for example, where most of the winemakers go surfing every morning ('You want to visit the winery at 8 o'clock in the morning? No worries, I'll have been up for hours by then.'), where the local town is a nice mix of surfies, artists, eco-crusties and Bentley-driving winery owners, and where it feels like you can get a decent meal almost wherever you go.

It's not just me who goes all moist and fluffy about Margaret River, honest. The region is crawling with new wineries and big vineyard developments: both Evans and Tate and Howard Park, previously important companies in the Swan and Great Southern respectively, have moved their winemaking operations here, while new labels seem to be cropping up all the time – there are now well over fifty Margaret River producers – and established wineries like Xanadu have successfully become much larger public companies.

Hard to believe, really, that thirty-five years ago this was a remote,

David Hohnen,
vigneron,
Cape Mentelle

isolated collection of farming communities, almost unknown to anybody outside Perth, let alone the rest of the world. When John Gladstone's now-famous report on potential Western Australian wine regions came out in the 1960s strongly in favour of this part of the world, a gigantic leap of faith was required to share his vision. But a few pioneers did leap – people like the Cullens (at Cullen), Tom Cullity (at Vasse Felix), the Pannells (at Moss Wood) and the Hohnens (at Cape Mentelle), and their faith quickly paid off: Margaret River cabernets in particular were all the rage in the late 1970s and early 80s, with Cape Mentelle winning the hugely hyped Jimmy Watson trophy at the Melbourne wine show twice, in 1983 and 84 – an (almost) unheard-of feat. What's more, as those mostly unirrigated pioneer vineyards and the ones that followed gain maturity, the wines they produce are getting better and better.

Margaret River as a whole benefits from the cooling effect of the sea: it is often erroneously referred to as a cool-climate region, but if you took away the moderating effect of the sea, you'd be left with quite warm growing conditions (even with the sea breezes, it's not what you'd exactly call cool here). Growers and makers have had enough experience of the region now, though, to be putting a fairly strong case forward for sub-regional differences. The wineries themselves are grouped into three main areas along the length of the Bussell Highway: scattered in to the south of Dunsborough up on the coast overlooking Geographe Bay (Lenton Brae, Amberley, Happ's etc.), huddled in extremely close proximity to each other in the Willyabrup area a little to the south again (Cullen, Moss Wood, Vasse Felix, etc.) and then bunched up south east of Margaret River itself (Cape Mentelle, Leeuwin Estate, Xanadu, Voyager, etc.).

Much of the newer vineyard development is somewhere else again: at warm Jindong, a fair way inland in the north of the region (and therefore warmer), and around Karridale, right down south (and therefore cooler). Bearing all this in mind, it probably won't come as a surprise to find that

Denis and Tricia Horgan (on the left), vignerons, John Brocksopp (seated), viticulturist, Bob Cartwright (standing far right), winemaker, Leeuwin Estate

Vanya (left) and Di Cullen (right), vignerons, Cullen Wines

...flavours of lemons, pineapple rind, grapefruit, hazelnuts – sorry, there I go again.

Keith Mugford, winemaker, Moss Wood

cabernet, for example, the region's standout red grape, can be much rounder, fuller, more mulberry-like at Willyabrup and have leaner, leafier, more elegant flavours south of Margaret River.

As the region develops, you'll probably see a polarisation of styles: reliable, consistent blends of the various sub-regions appearing as less expensive Margaret River wines, with the top of the market price-wise devoted to single-vineyard, or distinctly sub-regional wines.

Whatever. It'll still be absolute heaven on earth.

Margaret River flavours

Here we go again. Like Coonawarra, cabernet, cabernet and more cabernet is all you ever seem to hear about when the subject turns to Margaret River. Sure, there's more of it planted here than any other grape variety, and sure, when it's good it makes the best cabernet in Australia (did I say that?), but that's no reason to overlook the other things that Margaret River does well.

Take chardonnay, for example. From the exceptionally good sites like Leeuwin Estate, Moss Wood, Pierro, Cullen and others, and in the exceptionally fine winemaking hands of Bob Cartwright, Keith Mugford, Mike Peterkin and Vanya Cullen, the chardonnay produced here can be simply magical: powerfully intense and concentrated, but with incredible restraint and finesse, with flavours of lemons, pineapple rind, grapefruit, hazelnuts – sorry, there I go again. These are all deservedly expensive wines.

But don't let the quality of the chardonnay from this part of the world distract you from Margaret River's other great wine style, the semillon–sauvignon blanc blend. Either in an ultra-juicy, passionfruit pulpy way in the essentially unwooded wines of Cape Mentelle, Lenton Brae and others, or in a more serious, subtle, barrel-fermented way in the wines of Cullen and the new, superbly titled Suckfizzle, there's a chloro-phyll-fresh appeal to these wines that is entrancing. Verdelho and chenin blanc from this part of the world can share some of that attractive fresh herbaceousness.

Now let's lead up to the cabernet gently, shall we? Margaret River pinot noir has its supporters, and I'm not sure whether I'm one of them or not. Sometimes I like the rather hard, dense flavours in the top wines (from Cullen and Moss Wood, usually), but sometimes I'd like to see more subtlety and finesse. The region's shiraz has even more supporters, and this time I'm definitely one of them: Cape Mentelle, Sandalford, Willespie, Rosabrook and Serventy have all made some stunningly spicy, intense, dark cherry and pepper flavoured wines over the years.

Cape Mentelle's experiments with an old clone of mourvedre from the Swan Valley and grenache, dry-grown in particularly gravelly soil near the sea, point to even more excitement with earth wines in the future. Cape Mentelle's success with zinfandel has also prompted others to plant the variety, while Erl Happ's continued experiments with a whole host of other Mediterranean red varieties will take the region even further out into the unknown.

Which leaves cabernet sauvignon and merlot, more often than not blended together, along with dashes of their stable mates, cabernet franc and petit verdot. Again, the best low-yielding vines, dry-grown in the best gravelly soils of the region, produce some stunning wines, especially if they're aged (as they usually are) in the finest French oak barrels money can buy. The top wines from Cullen, Cape Mentelle, Moss Wood, Vasse Felix, Voyager and Xanadu have incredible depth of black fruit flavours, firm but supple tannins and extraordinary length. Margaret River cabernets used to have a noticeable edge of leafiness about them, and occasionally they still do, but as the vines mature, that is pushed further into the background by this riper, darker, more solid fruit.

Pemberton

Some predictions can come back to haunt you. In the early 1990s, I was one of the first wine hacks in the eastern states to write about the then little-known Pemberton region that was emerging half-way between the already established Margaret River and Great Southern areas in Western Australia. Back then, flushed with the scoop-like feel of the story (that's how I saw it, anyway), I grandly announced that the name of Pemberton would one day become as famous as Coonawarra.

Hmmm. This now haunts me for two reasons. First, while the early wines from Pemberton pioneers like Salitage were extremely good, and the latest wines from Pemberton newcomer Picardy are excellent, many of the wines released in between have been rather patchy (it can be a struggle for grape growers in the more fertile parts of the region to keep their yields down, and if they don't the wines can lack concentration and length).

My grand prediction also haunts me because it may have been more accurate than I intended it to be.

Some Pemberton vignerons like John Horgan at Salitage (the brother of Denis Horgan at Leeuwin Estate in Margaret River) and Bill Pannell at Picardy (the founder of Moss Wood, also in Margaret River) are convinced that chardonnay and pinot noir are the best varieties for the region. The first wines to emerge backed this up, too: they were deliciously complex, and quite burgundian in style.

Other, more recent arrivals, though, like Bill Pannell's winemaker son Dan (it's in the blood, obviously: Dan's brother Steve is a senior winemaker for BRL Hardy in South Australia) and Brian Croser of Petaluma, who bought the Pemberton winery Smithbrook a few years ago, are convinced that fuller-bodied reds are the future of the region: Pannell's plumping for spicy, peppery shiraz, while Croser's a fan of cabernet–merlot blends. See what I mean? Croser, cabernet, spicy shiraz, merlot, arguments over which bit of the region makes the best wines … sounds just like Coonawarra, doesn't it?

It's not, though. The climate and soils are quite different, for a start. This is magnificently rolling country, still fairly well populated by vast

stands of karri and mauri gums, despite years of logging. It has distinct sub-regions, too, with Manjimup the warmer, drier area in the north and Pemberton itself, a little further south, cooler and wetter. The soils in both regions are a mixture of gravelly loams and richer karri loams.

It'll take a while and lots of trial and error before the best varieties for each of these sub-regions will sort themselves out. In the meantime, enough people – including notable Margaret River producers like Cape Mentelle's David Hohnen and Moss Wood's Keith Mugford – are sufficiently convinced of Pemberton's potential to continue planting there or taking fruit out.

Pemberton flavours

I'm not going to take sides in the best-varieties-for-Pemberton debate, because I change my mind all the time. Chardonnay can be very good down here, in either the crisp-but-full, melony unwooded style of Chestnut Grove and Treehouse (Salitage's second label), or the leaner, reserved, more intense style of Picardy, or the much richer, brassier, more textural style of Salitage. But more recently I've also been rather taken by sauvignon blanc from Pemberton – both Salitage and Smithbrook under Petaluma have released wonderfully ripe, pungent, tropical-flavoured wines with heaps of personality.

With the reds, I've certainly had very good pinots here – usually in a rather gutsy, concentrated, plummy style – from producers like Picardy, Batista and Mountford. I've had some sensationally spicy, dark peppery shiraz with an undercurrent of (gamey) cherry fruit from Treehouse and Picardy, too. But the most fun I've had with Pemberton wine so far has been with merlot and merlot–cabernet blends: brilliantly elegant, intense red wines with great style and finesse (Picardy and Smithbrook stand out).

Oh, there you go. I've taken sides. Oops.

Lavender. I can still clearly remember finding this incredible smell of dried lavender in
the first glass of Great Southern riesling I
ever tried. It blew me away, too: it was so
unlike the limes and lemon zest and tanger-
ines I was used to smelling in riesling from
South Australia. This lavender experience

immediately told me that the Great Southern was different – that there was
something about the place that made its wines quite distinct.

I soon learned that the name Great Southern is an enormous net catching a shoal of regions in the far south of Western Australia down towards
Albany. From windswept Albany itself up to the Porongurup ranges and
Mount Barker, then across to the wide open country of Frankland and
down to the national parks and forests around Denmark, back on the
coast, dozens of vineyards are busy producing grapes and making wine.

You have to drive to the Great Southern from Perth down the dead-
straight Albany Highway to get a feel for how remote it is . You could fly
into Albany, but then you'd miss the cute sign by the side of the highway
just before Mount Barker which tells you that, if you'd flown, you'd have
been here three hours ago.

Its remoteness is one of the major reasons why the Great Southern was
not developed as a wine region until the early 1970s. People had suspected
it might be good for grapes for years: Californian viticulturist Harold Olmo
had recommended it for vines in the 1950s, and legendary Houghton winemaker Jack Mann had reckoned it might be worth a go years before that.

The boutique boom and a burgeoning market for wine in the eastern
states encouraged people to take the plunge, though, and in the early years
of the 70s Tony Smith established Plantaganet wines in Mount Barker and
the Langes established Alkoomi near Frankland. It didn't take long for
these pioneers to prove Olmo and Mann right, and over the next two
decades the quality of the wines produced in the region – especially the
tight, crisp, aromatic riesling and intensely elegant cabernets – encouraged many others to throw themselves at the mercy of the vine.

Despite their distance from almost anywhere and in some cases from
each other (perhaps because of this) the winemakers of the Great Southern

project a strong sense of unity. Considering the region's remoteness, it is also fairly surprising to find quite a few substantial wineries: Plantaganet, Howard Park (which recently moved its home to Margaret River) and Goundrey produce tens of thousands of cases a year, as well as contract making for a number of smaller wineries in the region.

These large wineries wouldn't exist if the region weren't able to support equally large vineyards. And this is where the Great Southern's contribution to the Western Australian industry is perhaps felt most keenly. I've lost count of the number of times I've been really impressed with a wine from a Swan Valley- or Geographe-based producer, only to discover by perusing the back label that the grapes actually came from Great Southern. Houghton, Sandalford, Capel Vale – the best wines that each of these producers makes comes from down here.

As a result, there's lots of activity here, with huge vineyards going in around Frankland and Mount Barker in particular. You may not see many more Great Southern labels in the future, but you'll certainly be tasting the wine.

Great Southern flavours

As you'd expect from the cooler parts of this big region, chardonnay can be very good: from Wignalls at Albany, Howard Park and Karriview at Denmark, and Goundrey at Mount Barker it can be really quite complex, savoury-textured, creamy wine with good lingering flavours. Plantaganet make a lovely unwooded chardonnay (sold under the Omrah label) with far more flavour and liveliness than most examples of this style produced elsewhere in the country. A few people do well with sauvignon blanc, too, in a very crisp, bracing style (Alkoomi and Omrah again are the names to watch out for).

It's riesling, though, that the Great Southern is deservedly famous for. The list of good producers is a long one – Howard Park, Frankland Estate,

Alkoomi, Plantaganet, Chatsfield (also good gewurz), Capel Vale, Houghton, etc. – and the style is, as I've hinted at already, quite a distinctive one. The best wines have some of the dry, steely austerity you find in Eden Valley riesling (giving them a similar ability to age really well), but there is a unique juicy, floral quality to the aromas and flavours, often with more than a hint of that trademark Great Southern riesling lavender smell. In some cases and in some years, when botrytis appears among the riesling, these flavours can have an extra dimension of ripe, apricotty fruit.

I find the pinot noirs from Great Southern, particularly those from right down south near Denmark and Albury, a logical extension of the WA pinots we've already seen: they started big and rather closed in Margaret River, became a little more supple and funky in Pemberton, and now, at the end of the journey, have lightened off in body but become quite wild and spicy (try one from Wignalls, or, if you can find it, Karriview to see what I mean).

A lot of people are getting very excited about shiraz down here, thanks to some medium-bodied but intensely peppery wines from Plantaganet, Goundrey and Frankland Estate (among others) and some atypical, heavily oaky wine show trophy winners from Houghton. I love the lighter, more peppery wines, and think the variety does well, but the best reds I've had from this region have been dense, herbal, complex cabernet–merlot blends from producers like Plantaganet, Howard Park and, in slightly more elegant vein, Frankland Estate (the 'Olmo's Reward') and Alkoomi.

left: Gavin Berry, winemaker, Plantaganet

right: Judi Cullam and Barrie Smith, vignerons, Frankland Estate

Size isn't Everything

Tasmania

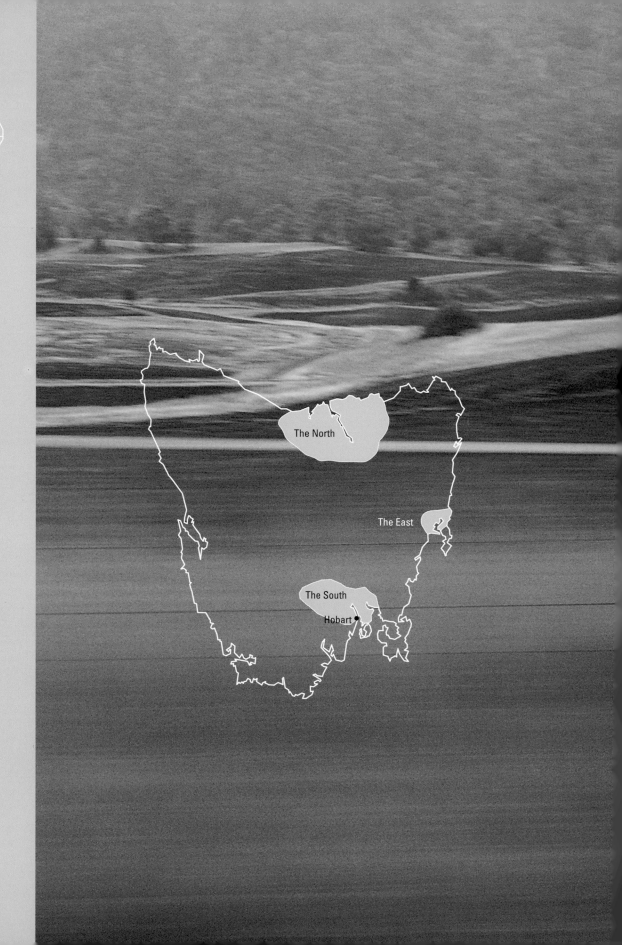

Tasmanian Wine Regions

The North

The East

The South

Hobart

You have probably gathered by now that I'm not all that excited by statistics and numbers. While some other wine writers and wine geeks get off on endless lists of heat degree day summations and rainfall comparisons and pie charts of sales volumes and graphs of vintage ratings, I'd much rather write about what a place looks like or what a wine tastes like or what I ate on Sunday. But I have to admit that the best way to get Tasmania into perspective is by grappling with some numbers.

Tassie is Australia's smallest wine-producing state. It takes only about three hours to drive from the vineyards up around Pipers Brook in the north to the state's southernmost vineyards down past Hobart. (That's less time than it takes to get to Margaret River from Perth.) There are only about 700 hectares of vines on the island, with only about 500 of those old enough to produce a crop. (There are single vineyards on the mainland as big as that.) And in 1999 those 500 hectares produced only about 3000 tonnes of grapes. (Which is less than a couple of the larger wineries in the Riverland would crush in a *day* at the height of vintage.)

But – and it's a crucial but – these 700 hectares and 3000 tonnes are shared by over eighty wine companies, with just one of those companies, Pipers Brook, accounting for over a third of the industry. Tasmania, in other words, is boutique winemaking gone mad.

Of course, Tassie wouldn't be quite the madhouse it is if it didn't make great wine. Not all Tasmanian wines are great – there are still quite a few poorly made chardonnays floating around, and the cool climate conditions can result in some pretty light and thin pinots and green, capsicummy cabernets – but enough of them are great to give the island state its top-heavy reputation, and to keep the madness bubbling away.

The madness actually began in the 1820s – before Victoria or South Australia had so much as a vine in the ground, let alone a wine industry to boast about. But the early flurry of winemaking didn't last (nineteenth-century viticulture wasn't quite sophisticated enough to deal with the island's unequivocally cool climate), and it wasn't until the 1950s that Tassie saw some vines again, with the pioneering Julian Alcorso establishing Moorilla Estate near Hobart.

The state took a big leap forward in the early 70s when Andrew Pirie planted the Pipers Brook Vineyard near Launceston after a global search

left: Andrew Pirie,
winemaker,
Pipers Brook Vineyards

right: Monique
and Steve Lubiana
(and family), vignerons,
Stefano Lubiana Wines

The North

Every time I fly into Launceston, the cool climate viticulture publicity people manage to turn on a real show. There's always a bumpy descent through thick clouds into persistent drizzle. The airport always seems to be surrounded by moist fog snagging on the hillsides. And there's always a bite in the air. It's not always like this in northern Tassie (we managed to catch a sunny – if windy – day to take the pictures for this book, for example), but it is like this enough of the time to make it a very cool climate indeed.

Pipers River, the first region to be planted here, is exceptionally hilly, very cool and characterised by its deep red volcanic soils. It's far more suited to the aromatic white varieties (exceptional, steely, long-lived riesling and spicy, fat gewurz from Pipers Brook, and pungent sauvignon blanc from Lalla Gully and Dalrymple), to sparkling (Clover Hill, Pipers Brook) and to crisp, lemony chardonnay and lighter-bodied, spicy, ethereal pinot noir from most producers (particularly funky at Delamere, intense and powerful at Dalrymple).

The Tamar Valley, on the other hand, situated further west, on the other side of the Tamar Estuary, is slightly warmer and has gentler, more gravelly slopes. Pinot noir from here tends to be slightly fuller, and cabernet sauvignon – in the right sites and in good years – can be very good indeed, in a fine, elegant way. Best producers include Rotherhythe, Holm Oak and Tamar Ridge.

The East

Despite being the most remote and one of the coolest of Tassie's wine regions, and despite the fact that there are only a handful of vineyards here, the east coast has a mighty reputation. This is mainly due to the exceptional quality of the wines produced by Spring Vale and Freycinet, undoubtedly two of the best vineyards on the island. Chardonnay, in a fine but intense style, with lingering flavours of citrus and creamy cashews, and pinot noir, in a medium-bodied, plush, spicy, cherry and plum style, are the best wines, although Freycinet have done well with cabernet–merlot blends in warmer years, and have high hopes for sparkling wine in the region (surprise, surprise).

Then again, remoteness is something that Tasmanians are just used to. It hasn't hurt the island's flourishing food industry, for example: indeed, the good name that Tasmanian fruit, cheese, cream, and fish already enjoyed on the mainland (and overseas) has helped introduce a lot of people to Tasmanian wine.

They are also, of course, logical partners. A hefty hunk of the quite extraordinary Heidi gruyere and a glass of ten-year-old Tamar Valley cabernet. A big chunk of just-caught pan-fried salmon with a glass of east coast chardonnay. A nice fresh chunk of goat's cheese and a young, bold pinot noir from the Coal River Valley …

I don't know about you, but my mouth's watering.

The South

Again, there are clear sub-regions down here: the vineyards following the Derwent River as it curls away north-west of Hobart, those in the Coal River valley to the north-east, those further over towards the south-east coast, and those around the Huon Valley to the south of the city.

Despite Hobart's sometimes uncanny resemblance to an English port (Bristol springs to my mind when I drive through the city, with its old pubs and stone buildings and steep hills), this part of the island state is actually home to some of its sunniest vineyards. As a result, some of Tasmania's fullest, darkest red wines are produced here: the bold, brooding pinot noirs from Stefano Lubiana, Winstead,

Crosswinds, Domaine A and Moorilla Estate, and even some fuller-bodied but still supremely elegant merlot (from Moorilla) and cabernet sauvignon (Domaine A again).

I don't want to give you the impression that it's warm down here, though. Far from it. This part of the world is still very much cool-climate country, as you'll taste if you try the incredibly tight, steely, fragrant dry riesling of Stefano Lubiana or Bream Creek, or the stunning sparkling wines of Lubiana, or the scintillating perfumed sweetness of the Wellington Ice Riesling made by Andrew Hood, one of Tasmania's most influential winemakers, and consultant to a whole host of the state's tiny vineyards.

Above the Granite Belt

Queensland

1 South Burnett
2 Granite Belt

Brisbane

Your mental image of Queensland is probably loads of sun and big blue skies and banana trees and endless stretches of perfect beaches and the Great Barrier Reef. Yes? Then it may come as a surprise to learn that not only does Queensland have a wine industry but that wine industry is also booming.

I know what you're thinking. Vines can't grow under full-on sub-tropical conditions, can they? They need cool winters and long, cool ripening periods to produce good wine, don't they? And you don't get that in a climate that grows mangoes and pineapples and sugar cane, surely?

No, they can't. Yes, they do. And no, you don't. Which is why Queensland's wine industry is located in the south of the huge state and a few hours' drive inland, on the western side of the all-important Great Dividing Range, away from the humidity and, importantly, up high where it's cooler and the autumn drags. (The exception to this of course is Roma, way out west, where it's stinkin' hot, the grapes often ripen well before anywhere else in the country, and the primary production has been port and rough red for well over a century.)

But the biggest explosion is rumbling away up in the South Burnett region, around Kingaroy, the town with the dubious distinction of being the peanut capital of Australia.

Vines were widely grown in southern Queensland long before it developed its strong Gold Coast/Noosa/Barrier Reef tourism image. Vineyards were very much part of the nineteenth-century settler's repertoire, along with orchards and livestock. Quite a lot of wine was sold locally and interstate throughout the 1800s, but by the beginning of the twentieth century, the southern states had come to dominate the market.

In the 1960s, a couple of pioneers began to make wine again in the Granite Belt, near Stanthorpe just north of the New South Wales border. Angelo Puglisi at Ballandean Estate, and John and Heather Robinson at Robinsons started what has now become quite a densely populated winemaking community, made up mostly of very small, quality-conscious, evocatively named vineyards like Stone Ridge, Violet Cane and Hidden Creek. For over two decades, it felt like the Granite Belt was the only wine region in Queensland, but over the last ten years the blast from the winemaking explosion down south has finally hit.

Wineries with ambitious cellar door operations have sprung up above the sub-tropical rainforest slopes of Mount Tamborine just south of Brisbane, some with vineyards attached, but most trucking fruit (and wine) in from the Granite Belt, and NSW, and even further afield. Other tourist-oriented cellar doors have also appeared – notably the remarkable Preston Peak, high on a mountain top just outside Toowoomba, east of Brisbane – again, with wine mostly being made and sourced elsewhere.

The Granite Belt itself is experiencing a renewed burst of energy, with most of the major vineyard activity taking place to the south of the existing plantings, down towards, and over, the NSW border into New England.

But the biggest explosion is rumbling away up in the South Burnett region, around Kingaroy, the town with the dubious distinction of being the peanut capital of Australia. This is big vineyard, big winery country. There's lots of money being poured into South Burnett. One day soon, a lot of wine is going to start coming out.

Granite Belt

This has to be the most appropriately named wine region in Australia. Hard, weathered boulders crop up all over this country, 800 metres high above sea level. You feel as though the vineyards and orchards around Stanthorpe and Ballandean are tucked in between the rocks, soaking up the heavy Queensland sunshine, then radiating it out again during the often bone-chillingly cold nights.

I know it's most likely a factor of the Granite Belt's weird, cool-sunny climate, but I can't help feeling that the region's wines often reflect some of this stony landscape in how they taste. Most of the usual varieties are grown up here – chardonnay, cabernet, sauvignon blanc, etc. – and in almost all of them I taste this hardness, and leanness on the end, right at the back of the palate. There's often a leanness that comes from the low alcohol: many of the regions reds are only 12 per cent or so, when most Australian reds are up around 13, and again this is a feature of the region's surprising coolness.

Good wines are made here – some very impressive shiraz from Stone Ridge, big and round merlot from Violet Cane and Mount Tamborine, an excellent sweet sylvaner and crisp, full-flavoured sauvignon blanc from Ballandean Estate – but there is still a lot of not-so-good wine. One encouraging development is the move towards non-mainstream grape varieties: Hidden Creek have made a really exciting zinfandel, and Tony Comino at Kominos is looking to plant the white Italian grape malvasia. Experiments like these may lead to some more distinctive Granite Belt wines in the future.

Angelo Puglisi,
pioneer,
Ballandean Estate

The grape growers of South Burnett – and there are a lot of them since the region was first planted about a decade ago – will proudly tell you that this part of the world enjoys a climate almost exactly the same as the Hunter Valley. Now I wouldn't have thought this was much of a recommendation (what with the Hunter being prone to rain at vintage time and everything), but I suppose what they're trying to say is that it's warmer and therefore more reliable than the Granite Belt, but not as warm as your mental image of Queensland might lead you to believe.

What makes this very attractive grape growing country is the combination of this climate and some deep red, fertile soil. In fact, keeping the vines under control can be hard, and reducing vigour and yields can lead to problems with ripening (again, not what you'd expect this far north). But if the growers can get it right, as some seem to be doing, especially on the leaner, greyer soils in the area, then some good wines can be made – wines like Barambah Ridge's rich, chewy cabernet sauvignon, and the new, clean, fruity white wines from Queensland's largest new vineyard development, Clovely Estate.

It's worth noting that these last two wines were made by particularly good winemakers – Bruce Humphery-Smith (who also makes the wines at Severn Brae, his own winery in Stanthorpe, and the Rimfire winery, south of Kingaroy) and David Lowe (based in Mudgee, in NSW). This is a key to appreciating Queensland wines: it sometimes feels like almost every good wine I've had from the state has been made either by Humphery-Smith, Adam Chapman (ex-Ballandean Estate and Violet Cane, and now at the new Mount Cotton winery), or Phillipa Hambleton and Rod MacPherson (Robinsons, Preston Peak and others).

It sometimes pays, I think, to follow the winemakers rather than the vineyards.

It sometimes pays, I think, to follow the winemakers rather than the vineyards.

Australian Wine Words Unplugged

A

From Aeroplane

to Zinfandel

The wine world is full of some pretty far-fetched and ludicrous-sounding terminology, and Australia is no exception. We can waffle on about malolactic fermentation, closed palates and vigorous rootstocks with the best of them, believe me.

But as well as the universal jargon that crops up wherever wine is made, there are some particularly expressive words that are unique to or commonly found in Australia. It's worth tucking a few of these under your belt for the next time you visit a cellar door or drink Australian wine in polite company. After all, you never know when you'll need to throw a couple of dog's balls into a flagging conversation.

aeroplane A big uncomfortable flying metal thing that takes young Australian winemakers to Europe and South America to make wine for British supermarkets. These flying winemakers are called Flying Winemakers.

Allen You know you've really made it with the Australian wine establishment when people start calling you by your second name. As in: 'I was at a tasting with Evans and Croser the other day, and Caillard mentioned that Merrill was …' I can still remember the first time Halliday called me Allen. I couldn't sleep, I was that excited.

ball tearer A really good wine, usually red, and usually loaded to the flange with alcohol/oak/flavour. Often accompanied by the words *absolute* and *bloody*.

barnyard What McLaren Vale red wines used to smell like before some bright spark realised it wasn't a regional character but the smell of hydrogen sulphide and urged everybody in the district to smarten up their act.

burgundian Strictly speaking, this means 'made in a similar fashion to how they make wines in Burgundy, using techniques such as hand-plunging a vat of pinot noir grapes, or stirring the lees in a barrel of chardonnay'. Occasionally, though, it's a useful word to describe overpriced piss-weak cool-climate pinot noir that I wouldn't drink if you paid me.

bin number For years, Australian winemakers have been obsessed with putting bin numbers and vat numbers on their labels. Originally, the numbers actually referred to the bins, or areas of the cellar where the wine was kept before bottling (Bin 95, for example, or Vat 1). Then they became code numbers that wine nuts were meant to follow religiously, as though they were in some cult (if I said DWB13, for example, you would immediately realise I was talking about the legendary 1973 Leo Buring riesling, wouldn't you?). Now, they're seldom used except on huge mega brands like Bin 65 chardonnay and Bin 389 cabernet shiraz.

blunnies Short for Blundstones, the classic Australian elastic-sided pull-on work boot. Essential if you're dabbling in a bit of weekend winemaking and you want to look the part. Along with a Drizabone coat, Akubra hat, moleskin trousers and a blue shirt.

cold tea A classic tasting term which refers to the liquorous, deep, malty aroma and flavour of that great old fortified wine, tokay from Rutherglen. Assam or Darjeeling, vicar?

counterjumper Another word for the nice young person who works behind the till at your local wine shop, and is always polite, informative and patient when you ask curly questions like: 'I had this wine the other day, right, and I can't remember the name but it had a picture of some sheep on the label. Have you got it?'

crush The Australian word for vintage, referring to the quantity of grapes processed, as in 'The 1999 Australian crush was 1.2 million tonnes.' Can also be used in the context of a winery's capacity, as in 'This winery crushes 100 tonnes a year.' The Americans use it, too.

dog's balls A stunningly good wine that stands out from a crowd of ordinary wines like – well, like dog's balls. Usually red, and usually loaded to the flange with alcohol/oak/flavour.

fruit-driven Used very often to describe Australian wines, or wines made in the 'Australian style' – with fruit flavours right up front and savoury flavours in the background. Some people don't like this term, arguing it makes Australian wines sound too simple, but I reckon it sums up perfectly that huge wave of flavour that floods your tongue when you drink a good shiraz or a great chardonnay. Fruit-driven. *Whoomph!*

GI Geographical Indication. It kind of translates to 'legally defined wine region', where the boundaries, climate, soils, etc. of that region have been described at length in a document that is then approved by a committee and put in some filing cabinet somewhere deep in Wine Industry House. Basically means that if you bring out a wine with Coonawarra on the label and it's not from Coonawarra, you can get into heaps of trouble. It's Australia's much milder version of France's Appellation Controlée rules.

grapetreader Winemaker. I made this one up.

look Taste. As in 'Jeez, Murray, didja see that new Bastard Ridge shiraz? You'll wanna have a look, mate, 'cos it's a bloody ball tearer!' (*See also* ball tearer)

old vine Like 'bush vine' and 'dry grown', you put the term 'old vine' on the label of your shiraz or grenache if you want to make it sound as though it's bursting with venerable tradition and concentrated flavour. There doesn't, however, appear to be any legal minimum age requirement for a vine to be called old. Which makes a mockery of the whole thing, really. (*See also* reserve)

ordinary You'd think this would be self-explanatory, but it's not. It's loaded with nuance, especially when accompanied by the word 'pretty'. As in: 'Gee, Murray, I dunno. I reckon it's a pretty ordinary wine.' A little less scathing, however, than 'interesting'.

palate cleanser A beer. A tradition. A way of life. After a hard day at the tasting bench, or a hard evening at the dinner table, there's nothing a winemaker or wine judge – or wine writer for that matter – likes more than to kick back with a couple of cleansing ales.

petrol or kero Believe it or not, good, mature (say ten-year-old) riesling can smell uncannily like Mobil's finest. If only we could buy ten-year-old riesling for just 89 cents a litre.

plonko If you drank wine in the 1940s and 50s, particularly in non-wine-producing parts of Australia like southern Victoria, you got called a plonko. Or a poofter. Or both. I like the word, though, and want to reclaim it. I reckon we should use it for Australian wine waiters, instead of the rather poncy term 'sommelier'. Just think. Instead of the sommelier's suggestions, you could have the plonko's picks. Has a certain ring to it, doesn't it?

reserve Like the bin numbers, phrases such as 'museum reserve' and 'show reserve' and 'winemaker's selection' have little connection to reality any more. Sometimes you see the word *reserve* on the label of a wine that really *was* made in limited quantities and/or held back for bottle ageing before release. You're far more likely, though, to come across the word on wines that you know are available by the tankerful.

slab Collective noun for twenty-four cans of beer, all done up in their pretty shrinkwrap plastic. (*See also* palate cleanser)

sly grog In the tougher times of the twentieth century, when the consumption of alcohol wasn't quite as socially acceptable as it is today, illicit sly grog shops used to flog cheap port to those desperates who couldn't resist temptation. A useful term I like to apply nowadays to that one sly glass of shiraz too many that manages to slip in unnoticed before bedtime and give you a thumping head the next morning.

suits The faceless backroom accounting, marketing and corporate types that scare winemakers in big companies witless and all too often call the shots in some cases. Not too far removed from that other modern wine industry word *shareholder*.

sweaty saddle What Hunter Valley red wines used to smell like before some bright spark realised it wasn't a regional character but the smell of hydrogen sulphide and urged everybody in the district to smarten up their act.

unfiltered Very trendy to have this word on your label. Should indicate that the winemaker has tried to handle the wine as little as possible, retaining good texture and flavour. Should not be used as an excuse for cloudy wine. (*See also* wild yeast)

ute Short for utility truck, and another absolutely essential part of the weekend winemaker's get-up. Trying to drive your BMW down a muddy vine row after a heavy rain can be an awfully messy experience.

wet dog Love this expression. It accurately describes the smell of a wine with excessive sulphur dioxide, but does so in a way that makes you think the wine has been shaken from a stupid, panting Blue Heeler.

wild yeast Another very popular term that you're most likely to see on expensive chardonnay or pinot noir labels. It means the wine was fermented by ambient yeasts – yeast cells that are floating around in the atmosphere – rather than cultured yeasts, which are added to the wine by the winemaker (the idea being that ambient yeasts produce more complexity and better structure). Wild just sounds better than ambient.

zinfandel A very useful red grape variety that every wine writer loves because it can be used to neatly round off a glossary with a big, fat, happy Z.

Index